Roadside Memories

Roadside Memories

BELOVED AND BIZARRE ATTRACTIONS
FROM NORTH AMERICA'S PAST

Justin Beahm

CRESTWOOD HOUSE

Roadside Memories

Beloved and Bizarre Attractions from North America's Past

Justin Beahm

© 2025 Crestwood House

Published by:
Crestwood House
PO Box 494
Marion, Iowa 52302, USA

Typesetting, Layout, Cover Design: Justin Beahm

Graphic Design: Lynn Amacher

A CIP record for this book is available from the Library of Congress Cataloging-in-Publication Data

ISBN-13: 979-8-9923886-1-9

Crestwood House and related logo are Trademark of Reverend Entertainment Reg. No. 7,747,229

Printed in USA

Dedicated with grateful love to Charles and Marilyn Beahm

Contents

Foreword

Remember those old Ford Country Squire wagons? You know, the station wagons with the faux woodgrain side paneling with the super cool, dual-facing rear seats and a backdoor that could either open as a hatch or swing wide like a door. Those wagons were meant for memories, as you could pack a family of 10 into one and hit the backroads to explore our country's most amazing landscapes, roadside attractions and thrilling theme parks.

Prolific author, producer and documentarian Justin Beahm takes us on a roadtrip to bygone days with his fascinating treasure trove of tales in "Roadside Memories," an entertaining column from *ReMIND* Magazine, now expanded with additional stories and imagery. Beahm's been part of the *ReMIND* family for several years, first serving as our guest editor for our special anniversary issue of John Carpenter's masterpiece *Halloween* (1978), and today as a monthly columnist. As a fellow Midwesterner we've bounded over our love of Michael Myers, TV and film's cultural relevance, *Happy Days*, the Wisconsin Dells, and beer.

Growing up, the Iowa-raised Beahm spent his childhood frequenting plenty of memorable attractions, first with family in his youth, and now as he wanders the world with his film work.

"I have always had a love for weird attractions and exploring abandoned amusement parks," he once told us, continuing, "I would love to unearth some of the stories behind those places that time has kind of forgotten, and it seems like it would sit well in the pages of *ReMIND*."

Today he continues that reverence for celebrating these pop-culture pantheons and all things monster related. His passion for places like the obscure Ackermansion in Los Angeles, Pennsylvania's Roadside America, Wisconsin's Monkey Island and so much more fills the pages of this colorful storybook. Many of these strange and wonderful places — where turnstiles once swirled with nonstop entrants — had tragic endings to their success, while others just never found the right audience or funding.

Beahm, whose house is filled with old postcards, brochures and souvenirs, endearingly brings these stories to light. Who knew Sid and Marty Krofft had an adventure park in Atlanta or that Bolingbrook, Illinois, once had its own version of Mall of America with Old Chicago?

Now it's time to stretch out your legs, fasten your seat belt, keep your hands in and enjoy Beahm's amazing thrill ride ahead.

Barb Oates
Editorial Director
ReMIND Magazine

Introduction

I have always been inspired by things found off the beaten path. Much of my youth was spent with family in Wisconsin on farms outside La Crosse (Mom's side) and in Wisconsin Dells (Dad's side) where I embraced the spirit of exploration and adventure in two disparate environments. The combination of experiencing rural life, where I would wander fields, mingle with animals, and climb around barns with my younger brother Mitch, was balanced by time spent in the Dells, "the waterpark capital of the world," that shed its commercial skin every winter to reveal new attraction wonders each summer. In both settings I bound myself to what made them unique, loved challenging my fears, and always found new alleys, groves, abandoned spaces, and unusual situations to revel in.

As Dad made his way through college he spent tourist season home in the Dells as a guide on the Olson Boat Company Upper Dells river tours, where he would entertain passengers with historical facts, point out iconic features in the river's sandstone cliffs, and tell bad jokes. At the end of every cruise Dad would hustle postcards to everyone on board as a way to make some extra money, a practice still in play with guides to this day, and I have managed to track down every season's card with him on it. Several even have his rockstar signature on the back.

Dad's love for the history of the Dells and my Grandmother's deep regional roots had a huge influence on me, and despite the town's endless offerings of contemporary thrills, we spent time there reveling in simpler joys. Outside of family, to me the Dells has always been centered around its natural beauty, Native American history, photographer H.H. Bennett and his influence on photography, and the intrigue of a place that leans into modern times while anchored in a bygone era.

There is a unique balance at play in the Dells where you can split your time between the world of theme parks, go-karts, and resorts, and the classic other half of town full of shops, restaurants, vintage motels sporting gorgeous neon signs, and two options for boat tours – the aforementioned scenic journeys of the Upper and Lower Dells, and the famous amphibious Ducks that weave through the forest before splashing down into the Wisconsin River. That intersection of the new and old was exemplified by the house my Dad grew up in, just a block off bustling main drag Broadway where I was always amazed by the quiet at night being in such close proximity to the perpetual noise of the strip where daytime shoppers were replaced by party people after dusk.

We didn't spend much time at the costly venues the world knows the Dells for, but did frequent a few attractions that continue to resonate in my heart. First there was the Haunted Mansion, a classic spook house with twisting corridors and intricate set pieces around every turn, safely held at bay behind glass. The Mansion's monsters, mossy cemeteries, Pepper's ghost gags, and dancing skeletons still delight me to this day, where not much has changed in one of the longest running attractions in town.

Around the corner from Grandma's house was our favorite mini golf course, Old River. Sadly long abandoned at the point of this writing, my Dad, brother, and I knew every inch of the place, through to tricks including how to use decorative course water effects to guarantee a hole-in-one in a couple spots. Old River was the one place we made sure to hit every time we visited, and I miss it dearly.

Most notable was Fort Dells, where kids would be martialized upon entry to help the Sheriff track down Black Bart and his dastardly Hole in the Wall Gang when not riding the train or miniature steamboat, feeding animals at the children's farm, rising to the heavens in the 335' Totem Tower observation ride, or watching Native dance spectacles. By the time I first visited Fort Dells in the 1980s, it was about 30 years old and already considered rather outdated by families accustomed to thrill rides and water coasters, but I fell in love with the place and relished every trip through its gates. It was a magical place where the young felt empowered with tin badges, and where we got a taste of grown-up life behind the wheel of vintage cars on rails. It made perfect sense, then, that I would choose Fort Dells as the first featured attraction when TVGuide's *ReMIND* magazine accepted my pitch for a monthly column about shuttered roadside treasures.

The relationship with *ReMIND* began in 2021 when I got a call from marketing maestro Mike Ankener, whom I had worked with on the theatrical re-release of John Carpenter's *Halloween* a few years before when Mike was with a company called Screenvision and I was part of the production company Trancas International Films. Mike had transitioned to *TVGuide* and wanted to know if I would like to contribute to that October's issue of their nostalgia magazine *ReMIND*. Before even hearing details, I was in. I had been writing for cinema magazines such as *Fangoria* and *Famous Monsters of Filmland* for years, but knew the opportunity for real estate inside the hallowed pages of a TVGuide publication would be next level.

I will never forget the first meeting with the *ReMIND* team. I am a film producer and at the time of the call I was in the wilds of Northern Michigan to shoot an interview with novelist Judith Guest for Paramount's Blu-ray release of *Ordinary People*. The forest cabin I was staying in had a no cell reception, so prior to the call I slowly traversed area roads craning for some signal. When the time came, I, and the oversized U-Haul truck I had rented (in this area rental cars were the stuff of myth), were parked on the shoulder in a clearing where I had two glorious bars to connect with. On Zoom with me was Mike, Editor David Cohea, and Executive Director Barb Oates. The energy on that call was infectious, and I pitched them on an expanded concept making the issue a wall-to-wall tribute to the *Halloween* film series, which they embraced. We delivered something really special that October in a magazine packed with fresh interviews and features spotlighting folks from all sides of the wild world of the Michael Myers franchise. The buzz around what we were doing was so loud it became the first issue of *ReMIND* the publisher ever took pre-orders on. It would also mandate a second run when newsstands kept running out, which was another first.

Throughout the *Halloween* issue process I formed a wonderful bond with the *ReMIND* team, particularly with Barb, who was always encouraging and kept the train rolling. A year later they asked me to return for their follow-up October 2022 issue, and my suggested *Munsters* theme went over big with the office and readers when it landed. Not wanting the relationship to dwindle, I reached out to Barb and pitched ideas for a regular column in the magazine, one of which was a look back at lost theme parks and attractions. That one she liked, and Roadside Memories was born with the inaugural Fort Dells entry landing in the November 2022 issue. Accidentally apropos, that issue's theme was wild west heroes, and the cover featured John Wayne and one of my all-time favorite actors James Garner. It was meant to be.

Writing this column is an absolute joy, gifting me the monthly opportunity to dive deep on places, events, and people that are largely lost to time. I get to put on my investigative hat, trolling newspaper and internet backwaters in what is often a lengthy search for as much information as I can gather on each attraction. I utilize news coverage, interviews, promotional materials, and tribute videos. I have tapped family members, social media groups, and friends for help and suggestions, and am eternally grateful for the contributions of all. While it can be hard to squeeze in with my usually intense production workload, Barb has been a patient, evergreen cheerleader and her support of Roadside Memories is what keeps it humming.

Over the course of the 27 entries this column has enjoyed as of this writing I have learned a lot about entrepreneurial spirit and the enduring legacy of even failed entertainment experiments. Every one of the entities, events, or places featured in Roadside Memories started as a spark in the eye of one or a couple people interested in doing something special. Something that would offer a unique experience that would positively impact the lives of patrons and offer them escape. Everyone highlighted in these pages stepped outside the lines and put themselves on a limb fueled by the simple belief in the value of enriching the lives of others.

By default, all these endeavors ultimately failed for what is usually a variety of reasons, but the story isn't about their decline, the part of each timeline I give the least word count to. At the hearts of these retrospectives lie bold journeys undertaken in the face of risk, often against the odds, and at great personal expense. Some resulted in the ultimate loss, but even in those circumstances the show usually went on in tribute to audiences and those who fell prey to unfortunate events. Pioneers possess a special endurance and tenacity that most clocking in and out of customary "9-5" jobs would consider reckless. I deeply admire these dreamers, and through this column they have taught me a lot about this world and the footprint we leave when we bid it farewell.

The history in these pages is that of our culture. The Hallenbeck-Wallace chapter sheds light on how dangerous and untamed circus life used to be. Circuses are now basically extinct, but when these fellows were circling their wagons, the big top was the most thrilling experience you could hope would roll into town. The Xanadu houses now look like charming artifacts, but you find they were way ahead of the technological curve, featuring communication and home entertainment elements we now live with every day and take for granted.

Westerns have long fallen out of favor with film and television audiences, but in their heyday places like Fort Dells and Ghost Town in the Sky gave tourists the rare opportunity to step into the boots of their heroes and experience a piece of the frontier life they were generations removed from. Similarly, wax museums are now a rare novelty, but in past eras they were the only chance to get up close to screen icons, and in the case of the elaborate displays at the Hollywood Wax Museum, step onto the sets of their greatest performances.

Concepts involving animals run from the wild to the outrageous, as was the case with the California Alligator Farm where visitors wandered around grounds teeming with gators and the farm's ads promoted the chance to let children ride the beasts. La Crosse's Myrick Park, a place I visited a number of times in my youth, gave residence to a rotating roster of sneaky monkeys that would often escape their confines and terrorize, or at least annoy, their human neighbors.

Unyielding artists are represented here as well, as was the case with the Gieringer brothers in Pennsylvania who decided as teens to create a miniature universe they never stopped adding to through the entirety of their lives with Roadside America. Wildly prolific sculptor Mark Cline's Virginia Monster Museum kept eliciting screams from those who dared enter his chilling abode, even when local "do-gooders" saw it as an abomination and burned it down. Twice. Multi-faceted entertainer Alice Cooper dedicated time when off-stage and off the golf course to start a restaurant chain that surrounded diners with genuine rock and roll and sports memorabilia they wouldn't see anywhere else.

Ideas like the "Crash at Crush" shocked the world when a promotional stunt to attract attention for a railroad's expansion became one of the most horrifying tragedies in rail history. Beloved children's television creators Sid and Marty Krofft took it upon themselves to turn a massive mostly empty office complex into a multi-story planet of its own populated with characters from their shows, then padlocked the doors after less than a year of dwindling ticket sales, mostly due to having not researched their location in Atlanta. But they gave it a shot.

Here you have tales of theme parks based on clowns, comic strip characters, the game of baseball, and a fantasy world full of pixies. You stop by a motel that drew lodgers with the promise of free ham, of all things. There is a lagoon turned into an adventure paradise with an early over-the-water roller coaster and a chute ride so fast it literally fractured the bones of riders when they hit the water. Some attractions lasted for generations and became screen stars in their own right, as was the case with the massive wooden Colossus coaster at Six Flags Magic Mountain in Valencia, California which made regular appearances in movies and on television.

The daring of these inventors was always on display, as was the case with the ever-expanding Dreamland at New York's Coney Island, which played by no rules, offering attendees some truly wild rides, interactive displays, and an entire micro city (complete with its own government) to explore. Disney Imagineers turned the fantasy cinema masterpiece *20,000 Leagues Under the Sea* into a ride where you boarded the Nautilus submarine and were taken through the treacherous underwater world originally envisioned by H.G. Wells.

I hope you not only enjoy a look back at places you may have fond memories of, but also mine inspiration from the experiments that led to it all. Collectively this is a book about creative bravery and how much we can all do with our own hands and hearts if we insist our dreams should become reality.

Outside of the two-page Ackermansion piece in the double Sci-fi issue, I have always had to work with a 500-word limit in order for Roadside Memories to fit into its usual one-page footprint, and while I enjoy the challenge of streamlining a story, I often find myself lamenting the material left out. There is always more than what I have room for, and with this compilation volume I am taking the opportunity to expand on these stories, pulling back into the fold the many fascinating pieces of each puzzle that initially had to be set aside. I have added relevant side stories, facts, along with a look at similar attractions or events in some cases, all in effort to present the most thorough celebration of the hard work and dedication the imaginative people behind these destinations put into their creations.

I would like to include a call to action for you, dear reader, as well. When considering how to invest leisure time when you have it, please consider locally grown places and events to invest in. As North American cities become more homogenized, where it can be hard to distinguish one from another when you step out of the car or airport and find all the same chain restaurants and hotels around you, it is more vital and exciting than ever to connect with locals and off-the-beaten-path travelers for the low down on secret venues, shops, events, and attractions that you might not have read about in travel pamphlets and on chamber of commerce websites.

There is vacation gold on this continent from coast to coast, you just have to do some mining to come up with the most valuable nuggets. As I have found with Roadside Memories and the rich history of the trailblazers who made it all happen, it is absolutely worth the effort.

I hope you enjoy.

Justin Beahm
January 2025

Justin at Circus World in Baraboo, Wisconsin

1

FORT DELLS

WISCONSIN. DELLS, WISCONSIN

1958 - 1985

"A goldmine of fun and adventure for everyone"

Original Publish Date in *ReMIND* Magazine

November 22, 2022

In the 1950s, long before Wisconsin Dells became "the waterpark capital of the world," the little town once known as Kilbourn was a modest collective of disparate attractions including The Wonder Spot, Deer Park, and the Tommy Bartlett water ski show. As the decade drew to a close the budding tourism industry was growing by leaps and bounds. Traffic was flowing smoother than ever courtesy of a new "million-dollar bridge" spanning the river near the dam, a roll of upstart resorts, shops, and tourist stops were steadily cropping up, and developers were dreaming of bigger and bolder ways to thrill visitors.

In 1958 ground broke on Fort Dells, a new attraction ideally positioned at the intersection of highways 12 and 23 near the ballyhooed bridge, an endeavor poised to become one of the most beloved family vacation spots in the Midwest. Modeled after Disneyland's Frontierland, the 11-acre park

Kilbourn & Western Railroad

was a western family adventure experience, built to the tune of $385k by the Dells Associated Boat Lines company and broken up into different territories.

Adventureland offered stagecoach rides, a trip on the Kilbourn & Western Railroad, a relaxing float on a mini paddleboat making rounds on the River of Adventure, and turns behind the wheel of genuine 1906 Maxwell and 1910 Ford cars on rail-guided roads. On an island in the middle of the park sat a Native American teepee and wigwam village where dance performances and a museum provided informative fun, and the Children's Farm area had a suspension bridge, petting zoo, and mysterious cave to explore.

The 10,000 visitors who crossed the Fort Dells threshold on opening day of July 18, 1959 were treated to an appearance by actor Hugh O'Brian,

Black Bart Hold-Up

star of the television western *The Life and Legend of Wyatt Earp*. While children were wowed by the rides and colorful gardens, the memory sure to be fondest on that day and every day after was the visit to Frontierland. The heart of Fort Dells, Frontierland was where kids were drawn into an immersive wild west action sce- nario by the fort's Marshall, played for many summers by Dells high school teacher Al Horn. After witnessing a bank robbery, the Marshall would deputize all willing youngsters, en- listing them to help in his hunt for the dastardly Black Bart. Bart, first played by Buster Reinboldt, then Greg Zastava (who held his very real wedding cer- emony at the park) became a Fort Dells icon, running around fumbling through crimes with his Hole In the Wall Gang as excited little ones chased them around blowing their cover. The Fort Dells "Jr Marshall" badges remain treasured keepsakes for generations of cowboys and cowgirls who will always remember helping throw the bad guys in jail.

3

Over the proceeding years Fort Dells would grow to include a haunted house and Totem Tower, a casual ride that took patrons 335' in the air for a rotating panoramic view of the area. While Fort Dells would often suffer the flooding of nearby Hulbert Creek, and maintenance became increasingly cumbersome over the years, the park survived until 1985, by which time its western motif had fallen out of fashion in favor of more modern Dells attractions.

Kiekhaefer Queen Riverboat

A strip mall now sits in the footprint of the park, but the past has not been lost, as the group Friends of Fort Dells erected a sign in front of the McDonald's on the corner in 2003 paying tribute to the bygone attraction. In a similarly loving nod the restaurant also sports a frontier theme.

FEATURES AND RIDES

Totem Tower Ride
Dells Fargo Stagecoach Ride
Antique Car Ride
Timber Trail Ride
Haunted House Tour
Big Bonanza Gold Mine Tour
Kiekhaeder Queen Riverboat Ride
Kilbourn & Western Railroad Trip
Indian Dances
Suspension Bridge
Children's Farm

FRONTIER LAND
United States Cavalry Troop Headquarters
Silver Dollar Restaurant
Trading Post
Frontier Fashion Store
Escape Tunnel

INDIAN LAND
Authentic Sioux Indian Teepee
Wigwams
Winnebago Crafts, Silvermaking, Basket Making
Injun Joe's Cave
Archery Range
Wisconsin Historical Society Museum

2

MOVIELAND WAX MUSEUM

BUENA PARK, CALIFORNIA

1962 - 2005

"An unforgettable thrill...to walk among the stars!"

Original Publish Date in *ReMIND* Magazine

December, 2022

The year 1962 was a big one in entertainment on screens big and small, birthing Best Picture winner *Lawrence of Arabia* and timeless classics *To Kill A Mockingbird*, and *The Music Man*, as well as television hits *The Alfred Hitchcock Hour* and *The Johnny Carson Show*. Americans anxious to stave off cold war fears found escape in vacations to Hollywood, California with hopes of finding recognizable filming locations and bumping into

famous faces. Allen H. Parkinson saw opportunity in those eager travelers and in May of that year he opened the doors of Movieland Wax Museum.

Touting his attraction as an opportunity to, "re-live great moments in motion picture history by seeing the stars of past and present sculpted in wax settings exactly duplicated from their most famous roles," Parkinson offered an immersive experience for visitors eager to step into the worlds of their favorite motion pictures. Celebrated Spanish painter and sculptor Antonio Ballester Vilaseca worked for two years readying the 60 figures presented on opening day, an event treated like a movie premiere and highlighted by the appearance of actress Mary Pickford.

As time passed the attraction would grow to include more than 70 scenes, enhanced by lights, sounds, and animation, welcoming patrons to spend time with Glark Gable and Vivien Leigh in *Gone With the Wind*, Humphrey Bogart and Katherine Hepburn in *The African Queen*, Nancy Sinatra atop her custom made motorcycle in *Wild Angels*, and dramatic setpieces featuring Vincent Price in his *House of Wax* and Kirk Douglas ready for battle in *Spartacus*. An avid art aficionado, Parkinson also presented the Palace of Living Art, a section of the budling on Beach Boulevard

in Buena Park devoted to masters of the brush and chisel, including a recreating of Leonardo di Vinci painting Mona Lisa among famous paintings and sculptures.

Seeing over a million visitors a year in peak years, Movieland Wax Museum grew to incorporate a walk of fame that included the cement handprints of Carol Burnett, Marcel Marceau, Ray Charles, and Ed Asner. As time passed and public tastes changed new faces would replace old, as Britney Spears and Kate Winslet found their likenesses next to Rudolph Valentino and Boris Karloff. A glitzy event welcomes each new statue and set of handprints making the tourist attraction quite the industry hot spot for decades.

Movieland Wax Museum would change hands several times over the years, and despite being featured on popular television programs like Reading Rainbow and in numerous magazines, waning interest led to the attraction locking its doors for the final time on Halloween day in 2005. Having survived over four decades and serving as home to the Hollywood's greatest stars, Movieland Wax Museum will forever be remembered as a loving tribute to the entertainment we love.

LIST OF DISPLAYS

Gene Kelly from *Singin' in the Rain*

Elizabeth Taylor from *Cleopatra*

Christopher Reeve as *Superman*

Metropolis Woman from *Metropolis*

Elvis Presley

Harrison Ford from *Indiana Jones*

Rudolph Valentino

Charlie Chaplin from *The Gold Rush*

Clint Eastwood

Cantinflas from *If I Were a Congress-man*

Shirley Temple from *Bright Eyes*

Jean Harlow from *Dinner at Eight*

Jonathan Winters

George C. Scott as George S. Patton

Abbott and Costello from *Who's on First?*

Laurel and Hardy

Buster Keaton

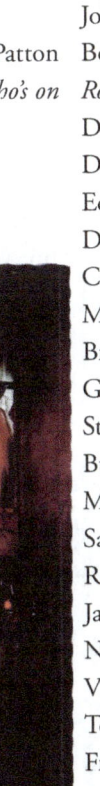

John Gilbert and Greta Garbo from *Queen Christina*

Mary Pickford and Douglas Fairbanks from *The Taming of the Shrew*

James Stewart from *Rear Window*

Lucille Ball

Leslie Nielsen from *Naked Gun 33 1/3: The Final Insult*

James Dean from *Rebel Without a Cause*

Liberace

George Burns

Charles Laughton as Henry VIII

Johnny Carson

Bob Hope and Bing Crosby from *Road to Bali*

Dick Clark

Dudley Moore from *Arthur*

Ed Asner as Lou Grant

Dan Rowan and Dick Martin

Carol Burnett

Marlon Brando from *The Godfather*

Brigitte Bardot

Gene Hackman, Ernest Borgnine, Stella Stevens, Carol Lynley and Red Buttons from *The Poseidon Adventure*

Mae West from *She Done Him Wrong*

Sammy Davis Jr.

Roger Moore as James Bond

Jack Nicholson from *The Shining*

Nancy Sinatra from *The Wild Angels*

Vincent Price from *House of Wax*

Tom Selleck

Fred MacMurray from *The Absent-Minded Professor*

W. C. Fields from *Poppy*
Gary Cooper
Charlton Heston and Stephen Boyd from *Ben-Hur*
Edward G. Robinson from *Little Caesar*
Yul Brynner and Deborah Kerr from *The King and I*
John Wayne from *Hondo*
Whoopi Goldberg from *Sister Act*
The cast of *Star Trek*
The cast of *The Andy Griffith Show*
The cast of *The Beverly Hillbillies*
Redd Foxx and LaWanda Page from *Sanford and Son*
Michael Landon, Lorne Greene and Dan Blocker from *Bonanza*
Fred Astaire and Ginger Rogers from *Top Hat*
Debbie Reynolds from *The Singing Nun*
Raymond Burr

Cliff Robertson from *PT 109*
Chuck Connors
Alan Ladd from *Shane*
Bruce Lee from *Enter the Dragon*
Tom Cruise
Kevin Costner from *Dances with Wolves*
George W. Bush
Mary-Kate and Ashley Olsen
Catherine Zeta-Jones
Michael Jackson
Michael J. Fox from *Back to the Future*
Liza Minnelli
Little Richard
John Lennon
Jennifer Lopez from *Maid in Manhattan*
Robin Williams as *Mrs. Doubtfire*
Keanu Reeves from *The Matrix*
Julia Roberts
Britney Spears
Jim Carrey from *Ace Ventura: Pet Detective*
Ricky Martin
Sarah Michelle Gellar
Cher
Leonardo DiCaprio and Kate Winslet from *Titanic*
Donny and Marie Osmond
Halle Berry
Barbra Streisand from *Hello, Dolly!*
John Travolta
Gloria Estefan
Bruce Willis
Jackie Chan
Chuck Norris from *The Delta Force*
Geena Davis

Madonna

Billy Ray Cyrus

Sylvester Stallone as Rocky Balboa

Arnold Schwarzenegger as The Terminator

Jerry Lewis and Eddie Murphy from *The Nutty Professor*

Bette Midler

LeVar Burton from *Reading Rainbow*

Elvira

Mr. T

Hulk Hogan

Eva Gabor and Eddie Albert from *Green Acres*

Roy Clark

Roy Rogers from *Don't Fence Me In*

Judy Garland, Ray Bolger, Bert Lahr, and Jack Haley from *The Wizard of Oz*

Linda Blair from *The Exorcist*

Lon Chaney as The Phantom of the Opera

Bela Lugosi as Dracula

Boris Karloff from *Frankenstein*

Lon Chaney Jr. as The Wolf Man

Ricou Browning as Gill-man from *Creature from the Black Lagoon*

Gunnar Hansen as Leatherface from *The Texas Chain Saw Massacre*

The Marx Brothers

The Little Rascals

The Three Stooges

Marilyn Monroe

Clark Gable and Vivien Leigh from *Gone with the Wind*

Bette Davis from *All About Eve*

Humphrey Bogart and Katharine Hepburn from *The African Queen*

James Cagney

Anthony Perkins from *Psycho*

Omar Sharif, Julie Christie and Rod Steiger from *Doctor Zhivago*

Kirk Douglas as Spartacus

Robert Taylor and Hedy Lamarr from *Lady of the Tropics*

Julie Andrews from *Mary Poppins*

Sophia Loren from *Two Women*

Robert Redford and Paul Newman from *Butch Cassidy and the Sundance Kid*

Macaulay Culkin from *Home Alone*

Tom Mix from *Rustlers' Roundup*

Ronald Reagan from *Tennessee's Partner*

Hugh Jackman as Wolverine

3

DOGPATCH USA

MARBLE FALLS, ARKANSAS

1967 - 1993

"Al Capp's characters come to life in Dogpatch USA"

Original Publish Date in *ReMIND* Magazine

January, 2023

Cartoonist Al Capp introduced newspaper readers to Li'l Abner and his hillbilly friends in 1934, initiating one of the most successful comic strips in publishing history that would span four decades in 28 countries. Set in the fictional mountain town of Dogpatch USA, *Li'l Abner* presented a comedic look at life in the American South, a first in the realm of "the funnies" and soon enough families around the world came to embrace Daisy Mae, Mammy, Pappy, and their hard-scabbled way of life. Capp was proud of Li'l Abner's success, but the artist couldn't have then known the popularity of his creation would eventually extend into the real world in the form of a treasured theme park called, appropriately, Dogpatch USA.

Newton County is nestled in the Ozark Mountains in northern Arkansas, a relatively rugged region where farmer and developer Albert Raney Sr. purchased a plot of land, then known as Wilcockson, in the early twentieth century. At the heart of the property was a creek-fed 55-foot-tall waterfall called Marble Falls, at the base of which Raney installed a trout farm that became a hub for area growth. With an eye on nurturing tourism, in 1949 Raney purchased and modernized nearby Wild Horse Cavern cave, re-christening it Mystic Caverns and opening it to the public the following year. The writing was on the wall: in the mountains there was money to be made.

Taking note of Raney's success was real estate agent O.J. Snow, who led a group of investors in the purchase the farmer's 800-acre plot of land in 1966 with the intention of turning it into a tourist draw. Tapping into the success of "hillbilly" television programs like *The Beverly Hillbillies* and *Green Acres*, Snow approached Al Capp with a proposal for a *Li'l Abner*-themed amusement park, and, ever the promoter, Capp saw the potential in the project and signed on. The team broke ground on October 3, 1967, and seven months and $1.3mil later Dogpatch USA welcomed its first visitors. Bringing Capp's vision to unbelievable reality, the town of Wilcockson was also re-named Dogpatch, Arkansas.

Earthquake McGoon's Brain Rattler   Photo by Cunningham

Populated with actors bringing *Li'l Abner's* famous faces to life, Dogpatch USA was a rustic wonder, offering buggy and horseback rides, an apiary, Raney's trout fishing pond, crafts, gift shops, and shows. In that first year the park would grow to include a railroad, surrey and trail rides, petting zoo and stable, and tours of the native grist mill. Anchoring the look and vibe were a number of authentic nineteenth-century cabins that had been brought in and re-assembled log-by-numbered-log throughout the grounds.

Following a disagreement among investors on profits made in the first year, in 1968 Dogpatch USA changed hands to local businessman Jess Odom who added a motel, campsites, a waterslide, and eventually sea lions and birds. Odom also arrived with a plan to attract off-season tourists with winter skiing at Marble Falls, the hill above the park, an idea that eventually drove the attraction into financial ruin due to the utility costs associated with having to continuously apply fake snow during Arkansas' only-moderately cold months. While the ski resort remained open for a while after the slopes were permanently closed, everything about Marble Falls simply served to siphon money away from the park below, and the first bell rang on Dogpatch USA's eventual demise.

By the late 1970s Dogpatch USA was starting to feel antiquated to families growing accustomed to high-speed rollercoasters and wild rides, also losing attention to nearby Silver Dollar City. When Al Capp retired

in 1977 *Li'l Abner* was retired as well, which left Dogpatch USA without a relevant gimmick. Despite attempts to capture tourist attention with celebrity appearances (including *Teenage Mutant Ninja Turtles* and The General Lee from *The Dukes of Hazzard*), Dogpatch USA limped through the 1980s and ended up padlocking the gates in 1993. The park's rides and buildings were left for Mother Nature and scavengers to claim in the years that followed. The land has changed hands several times since, most recently to Bass Pro Shops, indicating there might still be gold in those hills that once offered a uniquely comic-strip-branded family experience.

Grist Mill & Mill Pond   Photo by Covington

15

FEATURES AND RIDES

Trout Pond
Dogpatch Caverns
Peter Bella Grist Mill
West Po'k Chop Speshul
Convention Center
Frustratin' Flyer
Earthquake McGoon's Brain Rattler
Funicular Tram
Boat Train Ride
Hairless Joe's Kickapoo Barrell
Barney Barnsmell's Skunk Works
Slobbovian Sled Run
Li'l Abner's Space Rocket
Trash Eaters
Dogpatch Cabins
Dogpatch Auto Drive

PERFORMERS AND CELEBRITIES

Denver Pyle from *The Dukes of Hazzard*
Ike and Tina Turner
Reba McIntyre
Mary Sarton (poet, novelist)
Michael Murphy
Hank Thompson
Charles Shaugnessy from *Days of Our Lives*
T.G. Sheppard
Don Gibson

Wolf Island Paddle Boats　　　　　*Photo by Cunningham*

4

CHIPPEWA LAKE PARK

MEDINA COUNTY, OHIO

1878 - 1978

"Ohio's family playground"

Original Publish Date in *ReMIND* Magazine

February, 2023

Few amusement parks last more than several decades, but Chippewa Lake Park in Medina County, Ohio, lasted just over 100 years before quietly, unexpectedly closing in 1978. Nestled on the banks of one of Ohio's largest natural lakes, the park grounds first caught the eye of developer Edward Andrews who purchased the land to start Andrew's Pleasure Grounds, advertised as a quiet, scenic location for picnics and gatherings. Andrews eventually added a 100-seat sternwheel boat named Tom Sawyer for water tours, as well as a little roller coaster pushed on its track by hand.

Progress on the location shifted into high gear in 1898 when Mac Beach leased the land, re-christening it Chippewa Lake Park with grand plans to expand Andrews' core concept into something much bigger. Beach started with the addition of food stands and nightly live music, something the park would become famous for over the ensuing years. Patrons were delighted by bowling, baseball, fishing, and all sorts of contests.

Mac Beach's son Parker eventually took over as park manager, and with his arrival came more rapid development. A two-story building was added with dancing upstairs and roller skating on the lower level. "The world's fastest ferris wheel" drew attention, and in 1925 The Big Dipper wooden rollercoaster was added, thrilling riders with a 50-foot climb and descent.

After surviving the Great Depression and ups and downs in turnstile activity, Parker purchased the park outright in 1937 for $3,500 and continued to expand, attracting visitors with Kiddieland, the Tumble Bug, a merry-go-round, funhouse, and even a spaceship ride for tots called VX-3. A miniature railroad, The Kiddieland Express, rolled alongside the real railroad tracks that ran through the park, miniature golf, and two more rollercoasters were added, and a live animal attraction called Jungle Larry and His Wild Animal Circus offered adventure of a different kind.

Throughout Chippewa Lake Park's twists and turns, the live music never stopped, and the park became a "must-play" stop on tour schedules for heavy hitters over the years such as the Tommy Dorsey Band, Pat Boone, the Si Zentner Band, Glenn Miller Orchestra, and Pee Wee Hunt

who set a park attendance record in 1949. Pop music acts like The Lovin' Spoonfulls, Neil Diamond, Paul Revere and the Raiders, and Creedence Clearwater Revival kept hips shaking up through the 1960s.

A group called Continental Business Enterprises bought the park in 1969 with grand plans that never came to fruition, and Chippewa Lake Park entered a period of stagnation. Despite appearances by top national acts like Alice Cooper, Bob Seeger, and "Hollywood Death Cheater" Bobby Nolan, the park struggled to maintain steady traffic as larger, more modern parks in nearby Cedar Point and Geauga Lake offered more contemporary thrills. The 1978 season would prove to be Chippewa Lake Park's final, and without fanfare or public notice the doors closed for good at the end of that summer.

In the years since closing, the park's ruins continued to be a source of activity as a destination for curiosity seekers. A fire claimed the ballroom in 2002, and in 2008 a film crew lensed a low budget horror romp called Closed For The Season among the remains. While nature has re-claimed Chippewa Lake Park, the fond memories will resonate forever for those who paid the charming attraction a visit in its heyday.

19

FEATURES AND RIDES

Big Dipper
Ferris Wheel
Miniature Railroad
Carousel
Fun House
Tumble Bug
Dodgem
Little Dipper
Himalaya
Flying Cages
Caterpillar
Flying Scooters
Octoups
Tilt A Whirl
Rocket Ship
Wild Mouse

PERFORMERS AND CELEBRITIES

The Tommy Dorsey Band
Pat Boone
The Si Zentner Band
The Glenn Miller Orchestra
Pee Wee Hunt
The Lovin' Spoonfulls
Neil Diamond
Paul Revere and the Raiders
Creedence Clearwater Revival
Alice Cooper
Bob Seeger
Bobby Nolan

5

DREAMLAND

CONEY ISLAND, NEW YORK

1904 - 1911

Entrance to Dreamland, Coney Island N.Y.

Original Publish Date in *ReMIND* Magazine

March, 2023

On May 4, 1904 New York's Coney Island welcomed its latest attraction in Dreamland, a wildly ambitious 15-acre amusement park that would dazzle the world for just seven years before succumbing to one of the worst manmade disasters in state history. Real estate developer William Reynolds purchased the coastal plot between West Fifth and West Tenth

streets in 1903 and the first shovel found dirt in October of that year. Reynolds challenged crews of hundreds to work 24 hours a day to meet his aggressive opening day goal of spring '04, a feat accomplished despite persistent labor shortages.

Advertised as "The Electric City By the Sea," Dreamland aimed to outclass adjacent competitor Luna Park with a centerpiece 375ft beacon tower sporting one million light bulbs that offered a one-of-a-kind view of the region, the world's largest 25,000-ft ballroom, a pier stretching half a mile into the ocean, and a crown of eight pristine white towers spread throughout. Initial ticketholders could ride in gondolas through a reproduction of the Venice canals, take a spin on a carousel or ferris wheel, and perhaps most incredibly, visit Lilliputa, a "midget city" populated

MIDGET CITY, DREAMLAND

by 300 little people going about daily life in a half-size metropolis complete with their own government, police force, and a miniature animal livery.

Reynolds offered a wholly unique experience for tourists arriving by land or steamboat, specializing in thrilling views, harrowing scares, and the unexpected. Coasting Through Switzerland offered riders a trip through the Alps on Pullman Palace Observation car replicas, Dr. Martin Couney showcased his new invention the incubator, saving the lives of nearly 7,000 premature infants in the park over time, and every thirty minutes patrons held their breath as they witnessed Fighting the Flames, a six-story building bursting into a towering inferno, complete with hustling firefighters battling the blaze and stunt actors jumping from the roof in escape.

Not far from the arena where Frank Bostock delighted all ages with dozens of lions, tigers, and Blondin the pipe-smoking elephant, stood Hell Gate, the most infamous attraction in the park. Replacing a lackluster submarine simulation in Dreamland's second year, Hell Gate was a water

ride like no other, hosted by Satan himself who loomed large above the entrance. Brave guests handed tickets to employees in red robes and horned hats before settling into boats swept into what appeared to be a swirling whirlpool of certain doom, actually a spiral track propelling riders down a slope into a channel under the park and the sights and sounds of Hell itself.

Firefighters work on the Dreamland blaze (Photo: Library of Congress)

In a bizarre twist of cruel fate, it would be Hell Gate that would eventually reduce Dreamland to ash when on the night before the eighth season's opening day, some subterranean repairs being performed on the ride resulted in blown light bulb sparks colliding with tar, a combination that filled the tunnels with flame. Due to Dreamland's construction being primarily of highly flammable lathe, the entire property became a nightmarish blaze in no time. A recently installed high pressure hydrant system failed in the mayhem, resulting in hours of effort from more than 400 firefighters to tame down the fire that rendered William Reynolds' vision and 50 nearby businesses total losses. While no lives were lost in the tragedy, Dreamland never returned after the conflagration, but its influence on generations of amusement parks since is unmistakable.

FEATURES AND RIDES

Lilliputian Village
Hell Gate
Submarine Ride
Shoot the Chutes
Pompeiian Building
Electricity Building
Submarine Boat Building
Lagoon
Beacon Tower
Our Boys in Blue Show
Wild Animal Exhibit
Chilkoot Pass
Fishing Pond
Canals of Venice Ride
Doge's Palace
Coasting Through Switzerland
Fighting the Flames Show
Destruction of Pompeii
Thompson Scenic Railway
Orient Attraction
Filipino Village
Baby Incubator Exhibit
Pier
Ballroom
Airship Attraction
Seven Temptations of St. Anthony Show
Leap-Frog Railway
Beach

6

PIXIELAND

LINCOLN, OREGON

1968 - 1975

"On the Central Oregon Coast, where the weather is"

Original Publish Date in *ReMIND* Magazine

April, 2023

When Jerry and Lula Parks re-introduced Pixie Kitchen to hungry Wecoma Beach locals in May of 1953, it took the Oregon community by surprise. The 1930s-era cartoonish shack with a limited menu of sandwiches and pies had more than doubled in size into a colorful restaurant boasting a seafood menu of fresh locally caught delights. Ever the entertainer, Jerry Parks installed funhouse mirrors so patrons entering were greeted by a skinny reflection and the words, "you look hungry!" while exiting diners encountered a widened presentation of themselves in a different mirror accompanied by the salutation, "looks like you have had enough!"

In 1963, after hearing rumblings about a new highway bypass that would likely pull traffic away from Pixie Kitchen's location, Jerry Parks purchased a plot of farmland at the nearby intersection of highways 101 and 18 as a future location for his restaurant. Regional development was moving fast, and in 1965 Lincoln City, Oregon was born as the towns of Delake, Oceanside, and Wecoma Beach were combined into one. At the same time Parks decided to turn his recently purchased land into a theme park, and in November of 1966 he announced Trails End, a $2mil attraction with a western theme tied to the historic Oregon trail.

As landscaping of the marshy farmland was underway, Parks assembled his board of directors that included composer George Bruns and event coor-

dinator Tommy Walker, both Disneyland veterans. The park was rechristened Pixieland and construction was planned to run two years. A mini steam train called Little Toot was brought in to run around the park which included a playground, pool, carousel, carnival rides, and a gift shop. Also included was a 121-site campground.  When doors opened in July, 1968 admission was free and visitors paid only for ride tickets and food.

After a short initial season, phase two moved into motion with a crew of sixty workers laboring around the clock to meet the 1969 full-opening goal. New attractions included a log flume ride, western Main Street, opera house, and a dark ride called Gruniken Land in which animated pixies played in bizarre landscapes to the strains of a cheery song by George Bruns.

In its second season Pixieland would see 200,000 travelers pay a visit. Over the next few years, the park became a place of ritual summer employment for Lincoln City teens and an essential stop for traveling families, but in the early 1970s concerns about how the Northwestern coast was being reshaped to accommodate tourism started to flare. After President Gerald Ford signed into law the Cascade Head Scenic Research Area in 1974, the surrounding counties of Lincoln and Tillamook turned into protected national land and tourism dissolved. The park fell into debt, and in 1975 Pixieland closed after just seven years.

The train and log flume are still in use today at a park in Farmington, Utah, and a permanent display at a Lincoln City museum celebrates the undeniable imprint Jerry and Lula Parks and their pixies made on Oregon.

FEATURES AND RIDES

Restaurant
Little Tood Miniature Railroad
Log Flume
Paddle Boats
Grunykinland
Indoor Golf
Main Street Arcade
Picnic Area
Franz Log Hut
U-Drive Rides
Ice Cream Shoppe
Pixieland Palace
Phillips Candy Kitchen
Trailer Park
Blue Bell Opera House
The Shootout
Darigold Cheese Barn
Fisher Scones

7

CLOWN TOWN KIDDIELAND

HUTCHINSON, KANSAS

1957 - 1982

"Fun spot for the kiddies!"

Original Publish Date in *ReMIND* Magazine

May, 2023

Carl and Isobel Wanasek were schoolteachers in Hutchinson, Kansas who understood the children they adored educating. The couple also knew how long, and eventually boring, Midwestern summers could be, a problem they solved with Clown Town Kiddieland amusement park, which opened in 1957.

Situated on eleven acres of prairie behind the Wanasek's home, Clown Town Kiddieland was every bit a family operation, and Carl and Isobel were woven into the park's identity. Their daily presence, doing everything from manning the ticket booth to wowing little ones with the cotton candy machine, comforted parents who trusted in allowing their kids to roam free. The adventures at hand were many, and included a small-scale train, jeep ride, pony rides,  18 holes of miniature golf, and a merry-go-round populated by hand-carved wooden horses.

Prices were kept intentionally cheap so kids could work their way through a roll of tickets as parents enjoyed lei- surely conver- sation with friends, making the park a destination for all ages. Attendance would fluctuate from day to day, but the Wanaseks were said to be thrilled whether there were 20 or 100 cars in the parking lot.

In 1974, after nearly 20 years of running the park, Carl and Isobel sold Clown Town Kiddieland to Len and Billie Railsback, who added many new features including the popular pump 'em cars, vehicles powered by their pint-sized riders at first by a wheel, and eventually by a pump device. And then there were the trampolines.

The Railsbacks installed something unique in a cluster of trampolines that achieved the dual purpose of offering endless hours of jumping joy for kids and saving the park money by needing no operator, but the popular option turned out to be short-lived. As it turned out, the ride's quiet nature and easy access resulted in hospital visits and patrolling police often encountering and giving chase to sneaky bouncers at all hours of the night.

31

In addition to summer fun, Clown Town supported local stores with co-promotions, encouraged students by offering discounts for good report cards, and became a magnet for Hutchinson area teens needing employment when school bells were dormant. As amusement parks started cropping up around the nation with bigger and wilder rides, Clown Town Kiddieland kept its roots in safe, modest family fun, and remained a revered staple in Reno County, Kansas.

By the time the 1980s arrived, the Railsbacks were becoming over-whelmed with the financial challenges associated with running the park, as increasing insurance and maintenance fees signaled the end was near. In 1982, after a quarter century of entertaining generations of Kansas residents, Clown Town Kiddieland closed for good, but Len Railsback continued his investment in Hutchinson by stepping into the roles of local piano tuner and newspaper printer.

Clown Town Kiddieland managed to stay true to its family roots from start to finish, a rarity in the world of entertainment. Everyone who entered its gates looks back fondly on the little park on the prairie.

FEATURES AND RIDES

Miniature Railroad
Trampolines
Picnic Areas
Miniature Golf
Merry-go-round
Pony Rides
Jeep Rides

KIDDIE-LAND
WORNALL AT 84TH.
Fun Spot for the Kiddies!
—EVERY MODERN RIDE LITTLE TOTS ENJOY—
9c ALL RIDES 9c
6 for 50c and REFRESHMENTS 6 for 50c
4 ACRES OF COOL SHADE

8

COLOSSUS

SIX FLAGS MAGIC MOUNTAIN
VALENCIA, CALIFORNIA

1977 - 2014

"The greatest rollercoaster in the world"

Original Publish Date in *ReMIND* Magazine

June, 2023

Magic Mountain theme park opened in 1971 in the bedroom community of Valencia, California, roughly thirty miles north of Los Angeles. Situated on 200 acres of land, the attraction initially sported 23 rides, including two simple rollercoasters, Gold Rusher and Magic Flyer. Five years later the park made history with The Great American Revolution, the world's first vertical looping coaster. The new ride set the bar for thrill seekers and establishing Magic Mountain as a revolutionary in its own right. In an industry always seeking bigger and better, developers knew their next effort had to be something special, and in January of 1977 design work began on Colossus.

Conceptualized by International Amusement Devices as a blend of classic and modern coaster tech, Colossus was intended to be the centerpiece of the park, a sprawling wooden ride with a striking profile visible from the nearby interstate highway and that would greet park visitors as the drove in. With a support skeleton comprised of over one million board-feet of lumber, not only was Colossus to deliver fourteen exciting hills and two major drops, but the ride would also be a racer with two tracks running parallel with trains vying for first place back to the terminal on each run.

Construction began in August of 1977 to the tune of $6million. Just under a year later, in June of 1978, the media were welcomed to the park to meet Magic Mountain's newest monster. Television coverage included reporters riding the rails past workers applying the final coat of white paint,

and the reports were glowing, relating undeniably impressive statistics about the coaster. It was the world's longest at two minutes and thirty seconds in duration, the world's tallest (certified by Guinness) at 125 feet, it ran over 60mph, and sent riders into weightless orbit eleven times. Magic Mountain had done it again.

KISS in ATTACK OF THE PHANTOMS
An Avco Embassy Release
IN COLOR
Copyright © 1978. Hanna-Barbera Productions, Inc. All rights reserved. Permission granted for Newspaper and Magazine reproduction. Made in U.S.A.

Colossus was a colossal draw, and that proximity to Los Angeles paid off when Hannah Barbera was looking for an amusement park location for their live action film *KISS Meets the Phantom of the Park* (aka *KISS in Attack of the Phantoms*) in the summer of 1978. The entirety of the film was shot at Magic Mountain, a production that included two free concerts in the parking lot in front of Colossus and an epic battle between band members and some robotic beasts on and among the coaster's white support base.

Six Flags purchased the park in 1979 and initiated some renovation to Colossus, including redesigning ten of the fourteen hills to eliminate the negative g-force, adding air actuated brakes, and replacing the original heavy trains that had been wearing tracks down with more modern, light-weight carts. The rollercoaster continued to thrill guests for nearly forty more years before having its final run on August 16, 2014. In its footprint in 2015 the park opened Twisted Colossus, a modern ride that used some of its predecessor's iconic support structure to offer screams and laughter for a whole new generation of coaster fanatics.

COLOSSUS DETAILS

Cost: $6mil
Track Type: Wood
Length: 4,325ft
Height: 125ft
Drop: 115ft
Speed: 62mph
Duration: 2:30
G-Force: 3.2
Trains: 6
Cars Per Train: 6
Capacity: 2,600 riders per hour

FILM AND TELEVISION APPEARANCES

KISS Meets the Phantom of the Park
National Lampoon's Family Vacation
Step By Step
Knight Rider
Wonder Woman
The A-Team

9

CHAPMAN FUN WORLD

CEDAR RAPIDS, IOWA

1953 - 2001

"There's enough fun for everyone!"

Original Publish Date in *ReMIND* Magazine

July, 2023

Eugene Chapman was a jack of all trades. Between drumming gigs around the Midwest and East Coast in the 1930s, the golf champ earned his degree in physical education from the University of Iowa before settling into a string of job managing country clubs in Wisconsin and Iowa. His love for the greens was only outpaced by his love for the green in the form of illegal gambling and slot machines in his establishments, earning him a reputation among law enforcement and more than a couple late night raids.

In 1948 Chapman opened a driving range near his alma mater in Iowa City, and five years later teamed up with hardware manufacturing magnates Don and Aileee McIntyre to form Gene Chapman Sports, Inc. The focus

was on a bigger footprint in the local golf scene, and some land on Highway 149 (now Highway 151) in nearby Cedar Rapids, Iowa proved the perfect spot for what would become a combination 18-hole miniature golf course, driving range, and batting cage complex. Pro John Jacobs was on hand for Chapman's Recreation Center's opening day on May 22, 1953.

Chapman literally took his attraction to the next level in 1958 when he installed a revolutionary second floor to the driving range, adding ten tees above the existing 26 below. The same year a second miniature golf course, a par-3 golf course, and two archery ranges joined the lineup. He would open his course weeks earlier than others in the area in effort to please the early birds eager for each year's new season, and often hosted celebrity tournaments.

After a 1962 high-way expansion cut into portions of several of his golf courses as well as a section of the parking lot, Chapman and his team saw an opportunity to take a new approach to their business,

Chapman employees work on the rail carts (Photos: Cedar Rapids Gazette)

and on the evening of July 19, 1963, locals were welcomed to prevue Cedar Rapids' first illuminated golf course, crowned by 28 towering light poles that would allow play day and night. It was at this point that Chapman build himself an apartment on the property so he could tend to growing business demands at all hours.

Experimentation with attractions (indoor driving range, putting practice course) continued through to 1974 when Chapman sold the complex to his daughter Andrea and her husband Eddie Cole, a national trampoline champion. The Coles added a waterslide in 1981 and overnight the mostly golf-centric attraction became a magnet for families. In fact, other than the mini courses, the golf elements fell away by the end of the 80s when Chapman's Recreation Center was re-branded Chapman Fun World and a kiddie coaster, indoor games, space ball, bumper boats, and a never-ending lineup of contemporary thrills drew folks from all over the Midwest.

The site of countless birthday parties and easy weekend adventures, Chapman Fun World is forever etched into the hearts and memories of Iowa-area families who delighted in paying the diverse attraction a visit through to its closing in 2001.

FEATURES AND RIDES

Waterslide
Bumper Boats
36-Hole Miniature Golf
Spaceball
Trampoline
Batting Cages
Video Game Arcade
Go Karts
Petting Zoo
Pony Rides
Driving Ranges

10

GHOST TOWN IN THE SKY

MAGGIE VALLEY, SOUTH CAROLINA

1961 - 2015

"America's photoscenic attraction"

Original Publish Date in *ReMIND* Magazine

August, 2023

During the 19th-century, small impromptu towns were cropping up around the United States as the gold rush swept the country. Eventually mines ran dry and larger cities drew residents away from these increasingly desolate settlements, rendering many of them empty, and the American ghost town was born. In the late 1950s businessman R.B. Coburn took a trip through some Western states and was fascinated by the haunting sight of empty buildings and barren streets common throughout California and Nevada. In 1960 Coburn purchased Buck Mountain in Maggie Valley, North Carolina near Asheville, intent on creating an attraction that would bring the wild West back to colorful life. Ghost Town in the Sky was born.

Coburn's $1 million construction project started with the flattening of the top of Buck Mountain by bulldozing 45 feet from its peak at an elevation of 4,000 feet. No dirt was spared, and the relocated soil and rock was used to create plateaus connected to what would become the downtown

area and heart of the park. By the spring of 1961 Ghost Town sported more than 40 structures that comprised three different lands: Mountain Town, Indian Village, and Mining Town. The labor was local, as were the materials, pulling in 300,000 feet of lumber and 20,000 pounds of nails to create an authentic saloon, church, school, bank, and jail, among other buildings.

Seizing the opportunity to spotlight Buck Mountain's natural beauty, Coburn installed a double incline railway for visitors to take in valley views as they made their way to and from the park perched on the peak. Made up of 21,000 feet of steel that guided two cars that could each hold 48 riders, the 3,300 foot railway was an attraction itself, instantly becoming the nation's steepest with grades between 30% and 76.1%.

Ghost Town opened in June of 1961, welcoming families with its impressive vertical ride and immersive frontier experience that included an hourly gunfight downtown. Coburn's vision was a smash success, averaging 400,000 seasonal visitors by the mid 70s. Rides were added over time, including a merry-go-round, tilt-a-whirl, bumper cars, and dark

ride. The park briefly changed hands in the mid-80s, but Coburn bought it back in 1986 with the aim to add more modern thrills, and two years later The Red Devil was built. The steel rollercoaster's vertical loop, speed of 50mph, and 90ft height were only bested by how it seemed to send riders off the side of the mountain before safely depositing them back at the station.

After delighting patrons for decades, Ghost Town was in steep decline by the 1990s, and would open and close several more times before falling prey to financial ruin in 2015 due to expensive repairs, a disastrous mudslide, and overambitious owners that came and went, leaving unfinished projects in their wake. While it now sits abandoned and succumbing to the whims of nature, Ghost Town in the Sky will forever stand as a unique treasured family destination.

AUTHOR'S VISIT TO GHOST TOWN IN 2004

In September 2004 while wandering the Great Smoky Mountains National Park in North Carolina I made my way to the site of Ghost Town in the Sky, hoping I could find a hole in a fence to climb through and explore the ruins of what was reportedly one of the most unusual amusement parks in the East. As noted in the Roadside Memories piece,

Ghost Town is unusually situated on the side of a mountain, which I immediately recognized would make access a challenge. You could pull up to the entrance and get a good view of the vertical railroad tracks and carts, but that was about it.

I stopped by a nearby gas station to get some water and asked the clerk about the status of the park. She said it was for sale, and she introduced me to a fellow who just happened to be hanging around and who introduced himself as a long-time Ghost Town performer

as part of the downtown shootout show. Sadly, I don't recall his name now, but he was kind enough to make a call and, in a snap, I not only had access to the attraction, but also a friendly veteran tour guide.

Getting there was a challenge, as storms had ravaged the area in the years since their most recent closing in 2002, which left the access road almost impassable. Luckily my guide had an off-road pickup truck, and we were able to slowly climb over and around the trees and brush clogging our passage. Upon arriving at the top, I was

43

greeted by one of the most beautiful vistas in North Carolina, with miles of gorgeous valley rolling out more than 3,000 feet below. Surrounding

me were the bones of what was once the Queen attraction of Maggie Valley, much of which had been left to the same whims of mother nature as the road we had traversed.

Some rides had been claimed by fallen trees and foliage, others were overturned completely, and all were locked in a moment in time when, two years prior, the power had been shut off and employees sent home. The Red Devil Cliffhanger coaster track was showing signs of decay, and a group of its carts were at a standstill just beyond reach at the end of the boarding area. Not too far away from the rails I encountered a pavilion sheltering another group of coaster carts sitting in various states of disrepair. Similar to the coaster,

the vertical railroad shuttles used to transport visitors up the mountain face had been locked in place about halfway up the steep incline that once wowed riders.

The "Fort Cherokee" Western downtown was in the best shape, and it was fun wandering into normally locked off buildings like the the schoolhouse, bank, and church and visit their creepy mannequin inhabitants. They, too, are frozen in pose in an environment in stasis. It was strangely

congruent and there was a remarkable quiet to it all that belied the decades of family and machine-generated white noise, bringing calm to a place engineered for gunfights and screams of delight.

My guide seemed to enjoy revisiting the space and walked me through how the shootout used to unfold every hour. He regaled me with behind-the-scenes tales of real-life injuries to actors, accidental tourist mishaps, and the general day-to-day workings of the park. I learned about the ups and downs the site has had with ownership, re-openings, and closings. It is a place that attracts dreamers... developers who continue to see its potential but always seem bested by the financial weight of restoration and renewal. As I find to be the case with most abandoned amusement parks and roadside remains, there was a wonder to experiencing Ghost Town in its compromised state. It was as if the rides, buildings, and "townsfolk" were patiently waiting to welcome visitors  back, anxious to work out their technical kinks and move into motion again.

After an hour or so my guide and I made the perilous trip back down and said our goodbyes, both of us having had a memorable day in a place  that clearly continues to resonate with everyone who has paid it a visit.

Recent research reveals the park did undergo renovation in 2006, opening again on May 25, 2007, although with a limited number of functional rides. The revival was short-lived, however, as poor attendance hamstrung the effort, and the park was shuttered yet again in 2009. Various people and entities have approached purchasing and reopening Ghost Town in the years since, to no avail, so the grand Western dame on the side of the mountain has once again fallen silent.

Photos: Justin Beahm

FEATURES AND RIDES

Cliffhanger Roller Coaster
Bumper Cars
Chairlift
Sea Dragon
Dream Catcher
Geronimo Drop
Gunslinger
Incline Railway
Silver Bullet
Merry-Go-Round
Round Up
Monster
Miniature Train
Tumnbleweed
Mining Town Swing
Tilt-A-Whirl
Casino
Undertaker
Western Town Hourly Shootout
Saloon Performance Hall

11

XANADU HOUSES

WISCONSIN DELLS, WISCONSIN
KISSIMMEE, FLORIDA
GATLINBURG, TENNESSEE

1979 - 1996

"A foam house of tomorrow"

Original Publish Date in *ReMIND* Magazine

September, 2023

"We spend too much time overbuilding homes. All we need is foam!"

The words of Bob Masters, the man who hatched the concept for alien-looking abodes the world would come to know as Xanadu.

The seed for Xanadu was planted when Masters read an article on a group of Yale students building homes out of insulation. The ex-teacher was intrigued and started researching the concept, which led him to architect Buckminster Fuller, who in the late 1940s popularized the concept of spherical geodesic construction that would go on to become standard design for auditoriums, weather observatories, and attractions around the world.

Xanadu Wisconsin Dells

Masters first tried his hand at geodesic creation when he built a home for himself in Aspen, Colorado in 1969 by spraying foam over a large balloon to create a dome-shaped structure. Once the foam hardened, the balloon was peeled away to leave the egg-like shell behind. The bizarre looking 20x16 structure became the talk of the town, and Masters started making plans to market the design he touted as less expensive and more energy-efficient than conventionally built homes. It was time to show the world.

By the late 1970s Wisconsin Dells, Wisconsin had become the Heartland's premiere vacation hotspot, and when Masters visited he saw the perfect plot of land on which to plant his new promotional home atop the hill overlooking the town's main intersection. Teaming with designer Stewart Gordon, Masters took his Aspen design to the next level, expanding into 4,000ft of "livable" space, along with a silo-like structure out front. Balloons were once-again used for the construction, and polyurethane foam was employed to offer better weather resistance.

When naming the attraction, Masters considered the Chinese city of Shangdu, known popularly as Xanadu, the summer capital of the Yuan dynasty. Opening in July 1979, Xanadu would see over 100,000 visitors in its first three months alone.

Teaming up with architect Roy Mason, Masters next set his sights on Kissimmee, Florida near Disney's new Epcot Center. Mason brought with him high concepts of how technology could be integrated into daily life, and Xanadu went from home of foam to electronic wonder.

Mason showed remarkable foresight in his additions, including a central

Xanadu Florida

technological hub in the house that offered temperature, lighting, audio, and video adjustment via voice instruction. He envisioned computers connecting people around the world, a fully computerized kitchen, a greenhouse that cared for itself, and robot assistants. While the tech on display was actually a disappointing non-functioning facade, nearly everything Roy Mason dreamed up for Xanadu would become part of everyday life by 2023.

Xanadu Tennessee

49

OTHER BUILDINGS DESIGNED BY ROY MASON

Photo: Creative Commons

Star Castle in New Fairfield, Connecticut was built in 1983 in the style of the Xanadu houses, but was a home instead of an attraction. Perched above beautiful Squantz Pond State Park, Star Castle has outlived its more famous siblings and continues to attract attention.

The Mushroom House in Bethesda, Maryland was a for-hire project for Mason, who was contracted by homeowners Edward and Frances Garfinkle to accentuate their residential abode with his creative flair. Over the course of three years Mason turned the couple's two-story into a whimsical space fit for an J.R.R. Tolkien novel with mushroom-like "caps" crowning it curvy exterior and a woodburned sign sporting the name "The Shroom" facing the road.

The Darmuid Green House in Potomac, Maryland is an outlier in Mason's architecture portfolio. Situated in the Mazza Woods, the Darmuid Green House was built in 1987 and stands in stark contrast to the Xanadu, Star Castle, and Mushroom Houses sporting wood and stone construction and a striking splayed design that reaches for the sky with sharp, pointed rooflines. This residential home boasts nearly 10,000 feet of living space, five bathrooms, seven bathrooms, and four full-sized fireplaces to keep occupants warm in chilly Virginia winters.

12

THE ENCHANTED FOREST

ELLICOTT CITY, MARYLAND

1955 - 1994

"The adventure your entire family will never forget"

Original Publish Date in *ReMIND* Magazine

October, 2023

❝This is the adventure your entire family will never forget," trumpeted an ad for The Enchanted Forest in The Frederick News on August 19, 1955, just four days after the park had opened. Situated West of Baltimore on Route 40, The Enchanted Forest predated most all amusement parks in the United States and would go on to entertain generations for exactly forty years of treasured memories.

Howard Harrison Jr. was no stranger to creating a tourist draw as he initiated construction on a plot of farmland in rural Howard County, Maryland in 1954. He had helped his father Howard Harrison Sr. build and run the Belgian Village several years prior, a resort-style motel just outside Baltimore. The Enchanted Forest was born out of Sr.'s promise to his kids to being their favorite fairytales to life, a vision realized when Jr. teamed with local bank and business designer Howard Adler to join the nationwide trend of storybook attractions aimed at family visitors.

Utilizing paper-mache, cement, and fiberglass, Harrison and Adler worked off a generations-old list of fairy tale favorites that included the Three Bears house, Jack's 40ft tall beanstalk, the Three Little Pigs abodes, Humpty Dumpty on the wall, and Jack and Jill fetching a pail of water. Relying on the awe of childhood dreams come true, The Enchanted Forest eschewed mechanical rides in favor of incredible interactive experiences. Visitors who paid $.50 (children) and $1 (adults) admission could stroll through the iconic story locations at their leisure, stepping into the tales they had spent their lifetime with.

Open seven days a week, The Enchanted Forest didn't just transport visitors to the dreams of their youth, but also facilitated wildlife safaris to far away villages and interactive fun in the petting zoo and rabbits in the Easter Egg House. As time passed and crowd numbers swelled and ebbed,

it was Howard Harrison Jr who would walk from the family house down to the adjacent park every day with a pad and pencil in his hand ready to tackle his to-do list of repairs big and small. His four children would dress as characters and greet tourists in the early years.

Employing more than 150 local teens, The Enchanted Forest was THE Baltimore-area employer of choice for youths, some of which stuck around through the ups and downs the attraction experienced. Evelyn Myers and Bradley Selby worked for the Harrisons from the day the park opened in 1958 through to 1988 when the roadside classic started to fall prey to more thrilling attractions offered elsewhere.

Over the years the Enchanted Forest blossomed to 25 acres and would eventually include a diverse lineup of attractions including a teacup ride, a ride through the caves of Ali Baba ad the Forty Thieves, Little Toot tugboat rides, and a dramatic experience at the foot of Mount Vesuvius. By the mid 1990s the park went from a peak of more than 40,000 annual visitors to a mere shadow of that number, having changed hands and scaled back on its grand outlay. In 1989 the eastern side of the park was destroyed, and after a gasp of a final season the entire park went dark in 1994.

FEATURES AND RIDES

Mother Goose and Her Gosling
The Black Duck
Cinderella's Pumpkin Coach
Old Mother Hubbard's Shoe House
Papa Bear
The Giant Mushrooms
Gingerbread Men
Little Red Schoolhouse
The Crooked House
The Crooked Man
The Easter Bunny's House
Jack's Beanstalk
Giant Birthday Cake
Cinderella's Castle
The Caves of Ali Baba and the Forty Thieves
Teacup Ride
Alice in Wonderland
Little Toot Tugboat Ride
Mount Vesuvius
Jungle Land
Dish and Spoon
Willie the Whale

13

BOBLO ISLAND

DETROIT, MICHIGAN / AMHERSTBURG, ONTARIO

1897 - 1991

"The one day fun day for the whole family"

Aeroplane View of Bob-Lo Island Park, Canada.

Original Publish Date in *ReMIND* Magazine

November, 2023

Positioned 18 miles south of downtown Detroit, Michigan, Bois Blanc Island is an upscale residential community boasting rolling lawns and a dense tree canopy that occupy the footprint of what was once one of the grandest amusement parks in North America. The island, originally named Bob-Lo (or Boblo), is 2.5 miles long and half a mile wide, is only

Comet, Bob-Lo Island Park, Canada.

accessible by boat, and has been the site of a crucial conflict in the War of 1812, a transition point for ex-slaves heading for Canada, a lighthouse from 1836 until 1959, and eventually as an entertainment destination.

When controversial Canadian entrepreneur and political figure Arthur Rankin sold the island to his son McKee Rankin in 1869, the land was divided up into roughly 300 plots, one of which was eventually purchased by the Detroit, Belle Isle and Windsor Ferry Company in 1897 with the intent of drawing visitors for sport and relaxation. In 1898 a new ferry route traversed by the appropriately named boat Promise dramatically increased visitors and inspired the Ferry Company to buy nearly the entire island. In June of that same year Bob-Lo Park opened, offering an athletic field, baseball diamonds, a marina, tennis courts, and a bathhouse.

Three steam ferries replaced the Promise over the years: SS Columbia in 1902, Britannia in 1906, and the Ste. Claire in 1910. These magnificent ships boasted huge dance floors and beer halls in addition to breathtaking views for their one-hour trip from Detroit to Boblo. Occasionally used for

river and lake excursions, many visitors said their favorite part of the Boblo experience was the cruise to and from their destination. Entertaining the passengers for decades was Captain Bob Lo, portrayed by ex-Ringling Bros. Circus clown Joe Short, who stood at 4ft 1in but had a huge personality that filled every ferry deck with joy.

The park continued to grow as the auto industry in Detroit blossomed, and by the 1960s the island's profile included roller coasters, a ferris wheel, and other more modern features. Along with the new thrills came some gravely serious spills as the park struggled to keep up with maintenance and proper care of its growing number of attractions, resulting in a startling number of rider injuries that spiraled to the death of a patron in 1965. By the 1970s Boblo had developed the reputation of being an unsafe place where families were risking life and limb for a spin on by-then-antiquated rides.

The problems compounded through the 1980s, by which time Boblo had become the favorite hangout for gangs and bad actors prone to started fights during ferry rides and violence at the park. In the 1990s the park's owners attempted to breathe new life into the island with a marketing refresh and licensing deal that resulted in characters from The Simpsons wandering the park's grounds, but it was all for naught as turnstiles remained inactive. In 1991 the ferries stopped sailing and one year later the park was sold in bankruptcy, leading to the housing community that sits there now.

FEATURES AND RIDES

Carousel

The Screamer

Log Flume

Miniature Railroad

Super-Satelite Jet Ride

Sky Tower

Dance Pavilion

Self-Playing Orchestra Machine

Ferris Wheel

Safari Trail Zoo

Scootaboats

The Nightmare

The Wild Mouse

The Whip

Bumper Cars

Antique Car Ride

Miniature Golf

Cat and Mouse Coaster

Lighthouse

Flight to Mars

Round Up

Scrambler

Mammoth Slide

Pony Rides

Zugspitz

Fun Land

Umbrella Ride

Picnic Areas

Marina

Bug

Comet

German Restaurant

14

COUNTRY HAM MOTEL

BOWLING GREEN, KENTUCKY

1949 - ?

"Largest country ham display in the U.S.A."

Original Publish Date in *ReMIND* Magazine

December, 2023

H am. Not the first tourist draw that comes to mind when considering making a roadside stop, but what if it was combined with lodging for your road trip? James "Jimmy" Siddens owned a court-style motel in Bowling Green, Kentucky that was built in the summer of 1949. Looking to maximize his $15,000 investment in the construction of the property and give travelers extra incentive to pay his property a visit, Siddens made the unlikely move to make locally sourced meats his calling card.

Siddens knew the fresh highway bypass being constructed nearby would already draw drivers through the area, so his motel was perfectly situated to catch attention. To ensure there was no confusion on the matter, he named

his new inn The Jimmy Siddens Country Ham Motel, and handed out business cards promoting "fine gifts for now or Christmas" in the form of various meat options. Six-month, one-year, and two-year hams were listed by the pound, along with smoked bacon, sausage, and sliced ham that the proprietor would happily hand-shave for his lodgers. Orders were offered by phone as well, promising the deliveries were, "guaranteed good" and could be delivered via C.O.D. if preferred.

Approaching the Country Ham Motel was an experience in itself. Pulling up to the property you were immediately presented with a massive wall of raw meat hanging behind a huge glass window that allowed the curios to peruse the freshest offerings before checking in. Siddens smoked the flesh with a "delicate wood bouquet" to accent the "natural sweetness" mother nature already ensured. The wall of once-living cuts was promoted near and far as, "the largest country ham in the USA," and drew folks from coast to coast.

The motel behind the meaty museum blossomed over time, and by 1960 had grown to offering 14 air-conditioned rooms with tiled floors and electric heat. Guests were also treated to free daily newspapers, a transistor radio to help toil their visit time away, and baby beds if need be. Charging just three dollars for a single, five dollars for a double, and six dollars for a room with a television, Siddens made sure his generosity was met with a considerate price tag, making his motel an easy choice for single folks and families who all left with a postcard to ensure they never forgot about visiting the unusual stop over.

The motel changed hands a few times over the years, had additions come and go, and became the home for a never-ending rotation of unusual business including tattoo parlors, a market, and a tobacco outlet. Once the location fell into disrepair there were many stories around town about people looking to turn the once proud roadhouse into everything from a gentlemen's club to a drive-in, but in the end it spent the bulk of its post-ham years serving as long-term low cost apartments before total abandonment.

James Siddens' grand vision sat as an empty skeleton for many years before finally being torn down in 2015, leaving a hole in a town that locals look back fondly on.

THE WORLD OF SID & MARTY KROFFT

ATLANTA, GEORGIA

1976 - 1976

"Fantasy and fun have reached new heights in Atlanta"

Original Publish Date in *ReMIND* Magazine

January, 2024

Brothers Sid and Marty Krofft were introduced to American audiences at large in 1969 with an appearance on *The Dean Martin Show* where the boys showcased a lineup of dancing marionettes to the joy of their host. In the five years that followed the Canadian natives would become household names, having launched a costumed children's television empire on the backs of trippy shows *The Banana Splits, HR Pufnstuf, Sigmund and the Sea Monsters*, and *Land of the Lost*, taking young viewers into wild and unexpected universes.

By 1974 the Kroffts were approached by urban developers Maurice Alpert and Tom Cousins who were in the midst of pouring tenants into their $65mil behemoth Omni International building in downtown Atlanta, Georgia. While the massive concrete wonder situated on Marietta Street included a theater, restaurants, hotel rooms, 600k sq ft of office space and an ice rink, there was a very visible vacancy atop the centerpiece 8-story tall free-standing escalator in the middle of it all. The Kroffts were inspired, and The World of Sid and Mary Krofft was born.

Conceived as a multi-story adventure park broken up into themed zones, The World of Sid and Mary Krofft took two years to complete to the tune of $24mil and was thought of by the brothers as something of a testing ground for a grander theme park concept. They had already partnered with Six Flags at various locations and were thrilled at the opportunity to create an immersive universe populated by characters from their shows and beyond. They also aimed to best traditional thrill parks with an attraction that could be open year-round as opposed to just during fair weather months.

The World of Sid and Marty Krofft opened on May 26, 1976, welcoming visitors with modest ticket prices of $5.75 for adults and $4.25 for kids, guaranteeing it would take families no more than five hours to get through the experience. After being greeted atop the aforementioned escalator by two massive statues, guests made their way through Fantasy Fair. They then travelled down a floor to Tranquility Terrace where they could ride hand-carved unicorns and creatures on The Crystal Carousel.

Uptown was the next bold new world, putting ticket holders in massive pinballs that would be bumped and driven around through tunnels and incredible rooms as though inside a gaming machine. Lidsville followed, populated with familiar faces from the Krofft's weirdo hit TV show of the same name. The final endeavor is joining HR Pufnstuf in his battle against the nefarious Witchy Poo in Living Island Adventure.

While the park was certainly a singular entity, the Kroffts continue to claim its development was too rushed, and the resulting fractures in the plan became quickly evident as rides frequently broke down, and the notorious reputation of downtown Atlanta shooed off casual vacationers. After just five months The World of Sid and Marty Krofft closed and sat vacant, frozen in time, until CNN took over the building in 1987 and removed the various amusement installations.

Despite its bold outlay, The World of Sid and Marty Krofft left a mark on visitors and its creators. Said Marty Krofft in an interview years after closure, "this thing never dies for me."

FEATURES AND RIDES

World's Largest Escalator
Giant Harlequin Statues
Fantasy Faire
Tranquility Terrace
Crystal Carousel
Uptown
Pinball Ride
Lidsville
Lidsville Theatre
Celebration Musical Extravaganza
Mineshaft Elevator
Living Island Elevator
Costumed Actors Throughout

The World of Sid & Marty Krofft
A project of Krofft International, Atlanta, Georgia

16

OLD CHICAGO

BOLINGBROOK, ILLINOIS

1976 - 1976

"The world's first indoor amusement park"

Original Publish Date in *ReMIND* Magazine

February, 2024

Nestled in the heart of Bolingbrook, Illinois, Old Chicago once stood as a beacon of entertainment, blending the charm of an indoor mall with the thrills of an amusement park. This unique complex, spanning over 150 acres, left an indelible mark on the memories of those who experienced its magic during the 1970s and 1980s.

In the early 1970s, Old Chicago emerged as a groundbreaking concept, a response to the unpredictable Chicago weather that often dampened outdoor amusement park plans. This expansive indoor wonderland brought together the joy of shopping and the excitement of amusement rides under one roof. Families flocked to Old Chicago, eager to escape the elements and indulge in a day of wholesome fun.

Old Chicago Amusement Park

The centerpiece of Old Chicago was its indoor amusement park, a sprawling playground of rides and attractions that catered to visitors of all ages. From the classic charm of carousel rides to the adrenaline-pumping twists of roller coasters, the park offered a diverse range of experiences. The controlled climate allowed families to enjoy the thrill of outdoor rides without worrying about the whims of Chicago's weather.

Adjacent to the amusement park was the sprawling mall section of Old Chicago, boasting an eclectic mix of shops and boutiques. Visitors could explore everything from well-known retailers to local businesses, creating a shopping experience unlike any other. The mall was not merely a commercial space; it was a communal gathering point where families and friends mingled, shopped, and created enduring memories.

Old Chicago's architecture played a vital role in its allure. Designed to evoke the ambiance of a charming European village, the complex transported visitors to a different world. The distinctive design elements enhanced the overall experience, making a visit to Old Chicago feel like stepping into a magical realm where entertainment and commerce seamlessly coexisted.

The complex was not merely a static space; it pulsated with life through numerous events and festivals. Seasonal celebrations, live performances, and parades added to the vibrancy of Old Chicago, solidifying its reputation as a premier destination in the Chicagoland area.

Despite its initial success, Old Chicago faced challenges in the late 1970s and early 1980s. Changes in ownership and increased competition from other entertainment venues led to a decline in visitors. In 1980, the amusement park section was closed, marking a turning point in Old Chicago's history. The complex struggled to regain its former glory, and by 1986, it closed its doors for the last time.

The land that once housed Old Chicago underwent a transformation. The buildings were eventually demolished, and the landscape evolved, but the memories of Old Chicago lingered in the hearts of those who cherished its unique blend of shopping and amusement. It remains a symbol of a bygone era, a testament to the creativity that once defined Chicago's entertainment landscape. Today, Bolingbrook has moved forward, but the legacy of Old Chicago endures in the stories and recollections of those fortunate enough to have experienced its enchanting charm.

17

MONKEY ISLAND

MYRICK PARK - LA CROSSE, WISCONSIN

1929 - 2007

Original Publish Date in *ReMIND* Magazine

March, 2024

"In order to get people to come to La Crosse...you simply have to have something to show them, some oddity or something the like of which they haven't in their own hometown," said Alderman William Roellig in October of 1924. La Crosse, Wisconsin was already known for its rich brewery history and scenic position at the intersection of the Mississippi, Black, and La Crosse rivers, but as the 1920s saw the automobile changing how and where people were investing in leisure time, city officials were searching for new ways to attract visitors. Roellig's proposal: monkeys.

The idea was born when Roellig visited the Milwaukee Zoo and took note of the success of the "monkey island" there, an attraction that was drawing thousands of tourists in fair weather months. Roellig fingered Myrick Park, a popular La Crosse picnic spot near the river, for the location and local architect Otto Merman set about designing the primate enclosure which called for a 300ft outer wall in an elliptical shape surrounding a cement island. Separating the island from the wall would be a 15-20ft wide moat, with the promise of being escape-proof.

There would be houses made from rocks pulled from regional ridges and during colder months the plan was to house the monks in nearby greenhouses. Eventually the island came to include ferris wheels, some decommissioned power poles for climbing, and other apparatuses for play. Construction was paid for by the Veterans of Foreign Wars, and local brick yards donated 5,000 bricks to the project. The monkeys proved the nucleus of a grander plan for a modest, albeit diverse, zoo to include bears, wolves, raccoons, birds, and other animals. Thirteen cages were sent

MONKEY ISLAND, MYRICK PARK, LA CROSSE, WIS.—15

from the Ringling Bros Circus in nearby Baraboo, and benefit events like community dances helped planners cross the financial finish line.

The initial two-dozen spider monkeys arrived from Central and South America to the great celebration of more than 1,000 visitors on opening day of August 25, 1929. The problems, however, began almost immediately as the sneaky primates quickly cracked the code of the "escape-proof" island and moat, figuring out how to make a break for it via overflow pipes and creative climbing which led to regular headlines about fugitives being found in trees and atop buildings across the city.

Furthermore, inbreeding and violence among the monkeys led to continuous problems and portions of herds having to be sold off or euthanized time and again over the years. The initial plans for winter greenhouse lodging didn't work out, giving way to them being kept at the city pump house and eventually the LA Crosse Animal Hospital. It was from the Animal Hospital that the most infamous escape occurred in 1937 when fifteen monkeys snuck out a cracked door and wreaked havoc across town and at the power plant for days before recapture.

Despite injuries to the untrained staff, police officers, and visiting children over time, Monkey Island remained open until 2007 when the remaining primates were adopted out. Despite the frequent chaos, memories of La Crosse's monkey attraction will forever resonate with residents.

GREAT MYRICK MONKEY ESCAPES

9/22/1929 - Just a few months after Myrick Park opened, four monkeys bested the untrained staff and escaped from the zoo, making a fast track for nearby residential treetops. *The La Crosse Tribune* ran a piece on the situation asking readers for ideas on how to lure the monks down so they could be returned to their park habitat. This became a regular occurrence throughout that first season.

4/25/1930 - A news article reveals plans are underway to make changes to the Monkey Island enclosure before its inhabitants will return there from their winter home at the city pump house due to a number of primate escapes during the attraction's freshman season. Myrick Park employees figured out the creative rascals had overcome the "escape-proof" moat surrounding their village by jumping from overflow pipes to the fence on the other side of the water, then making their way to freedom. Officials decided to remove one of the pipes and relocate another to stave off the break outs.

7/23/1931 - Seventeen monkeys swam across the moat around Monkey Island, scaled the fence, and made their way into trees around Myrick Park. A group of county homemakers having their annual picnic reported being entertained by the simians who delighted the crowd with tricks and silliness. Zoo caretakers reassured the public they monkeys would return to their

home when they were hungry,
which is exactly what happened
a few hours later when feed was dumped
in clear view on the island and the sneaks
found their way back to feed and sleep as usual.

11/24/1937 - After a stray monkey was found in
the pattern department at Allis Chalmer's store
in La Crosse, authorities were notified, and
it was discovered fifteen hairy Houdinis had
escaped from their winter quarters at
the La Crosse Animal Hospital and
were making their way around town. A group of animal hospital workers
set out in hot pursuit, and while most of the fugitives were captured in
relatively short order, three especially bold tramps made their way to the
Northern States Power Company gas plant where they scaled poles and
equipment to evade their pursuers. Onlookers soon filled the street, watching as coconuts were presented to entice the animals, which eventually
worked, and all were transported back to their hospital abode.

7/3/1950 - Three monkeys escaped from Myrick Park and were reported
still absent three days later, a duration park officials said was longer than
with past disappearances that usually ended after a day or so when the
monks got hungry and would return. Those officials theorized the three
absconders were likely spooked by increasingly frequent fighting among
the Island's residents and fled to avoid the drama. Reports came in that the
monkeys were seen lounging around on headstones at nearby Oak Grove
Cemetery. *The La Crosse Tribune* advised residents on how to handle things
in the event of a home primate encounter, suggesting, "if the monkeys enter
a garage, all doors and windows should be shut, and the park department
should be notified immediately."

5/17/1962 - During the process of transporting the Myrick Park monkeys
back to the park from their winter quarters, one daredevil broke out and
ran away not once, but twice in the same day, ending up in a tree in the
vicinity of Caledonia and Rose Streets. A fire department unit was called
in to extract the evader from his perch using an aerial ladder and net.

18

THE CRASH AT CRUSH

WEST, TEXAS

SEPTEMBER 15, 1896

Original Publish Date in *ReMIND* Magazine

April, 2024

One of the most infamous publicity stunts in American history occurred in September 1896 when two locomotives had a head-on collision in front of thousands of spectators who traveled from near and far to bear witness to the spectacle. It was a one-time roadside oddity meant to promote the Missouri-Kansas-Texas Railroad's expanding network of travel destinations but ended in tragedy.

By 1896 the Missouri-Kansas-Texas Railroad (affectionately referred to as "The Katy") was on the move with a new route between Dallas and Houston, Texas that would allow passengers quicker transit between the two growing metropolitan areas. Katy agent William Crush dreamt up the idea of staging a train crash to draw attention to their efforts and bring in tourists to experience the comfort of their tracks and bear witness to something unique.

Crush's vision was born out of a similar staged event that occurred earlier that year in Lancaster, Ohio where the Columbus and Hocking Valley Railroad ran two locomotives into each other to the delight of more than 20,000 spectators to celebrate opening day of a new park. He pitched the concept to Katy officials who saw its potential and gave it the green light. The price tag for the trip to and from the site was $3.50 per person from anywhere in the state and plans got underway.

Pinpointing a location 14 miles north of Waco, Crush and Katy crews created an amphitheater complete with a grandstand, a large circus tent donated by the Ringling Bros. circus, a special train depot, and a viewing platform for media to capture the happening. The day would include lemonade stands, vendors, and a small carnival to accompany the crash.

The Katy had just purchased a fleet of powerful 60-ton engines, so the two trains destined for public execution were chosen from among the older decommissioned 35-ton Baldwin models that were now sitting unused. The fates of locomotives no. 999 and 1001 were sealed and four miles of track was laid for their final journeys.

The morning of September 15, 1896 saw a flood of tourists arriving with turnstile estimates totaling roughly 40,000 people. A test run was done where the two trains, each pulling cars loaded with railroad ties, slowly traversed their short runs, meeting in the middle for some photographs

Photos: Library of Congress

before returning to their starting points at opposite ends of the track. At 5pm Crush gave the signal and both trains, each with an engineer inside, started toward each other, the drivers jumping out to safety after a few moments leaving the speeding "bullets" careening toward impact at roughly 45mph.

The impact caused both engines to explode, sending shrapnel flying in all directions. Some of the debris hit spectators, killing two and injuring many others and all that was left of the engines was a tangled mass of metal and wood crowned in flames and smoke. Despite the tragic incident many railroads attempted similar feats in following years, thankfully none as deadly as what happened on that fateful day in "The Crash at Crush."

Photos: Library of Congress

19

BOARDWALK AND BASEBALL

HAINES CITY, FLORIDA

1974 - 1990

Original Publish Date in *ReMIND* Magazine

May, 2024

Walt Disney has inspired generations with his films, but he also inspired an endless stream of theme parks that popped up in the years following his Disneyland opening in 1955. It was just that source material Mattel referenced when they dreamed up Circus World Showcase. When Mattel purchased the Ringling Bros and Barnum & Bailey Circus in 1971 for $40mil they stepped onto the path paved by Disney, and with managers Irvin and Israel Feld purchased land at the intersection of Interstate 4 and US HWY 27 in Haines, Florida with plans to build  an attraction centered around a 19-story elephant-shaped hotel, an IMAX theater, and rides. The location would also serve as the winter home of the circus and all its animals. While the elephant hotel proved too costly, the 6-story IMAX theater inside a massive big top tent building served as the centerpiece of what would become Circus World Showcase.

The attraction opened in 1974, growing in following years to include diving and wild west shows, and a year-round elephant barn, and by 1976 Circus Word was seeing over a million tourists annually. By 1982 attendance had slowed due to the draw of the more advanced parks around Disneyland in Florida, and businessman Jim Monaghan bought Circus World from Mattel and the Felds for $10mil, auctioning off the older rides, adding nine modern thrill rides, and branding the park Thrill City USA. The new approach was short-lived, and one day in the spring of 1986 employees showed up to work to find the park was closed with no advance notice.

Monaghan sold the park to publishing giant Harcourt Brace Jovanovich (HBJ) who closed the venue for months as they re-tooled the attraction, adopting the vibe, colors, and decorative flair of East coast seaside theme parks such as Coney Island, but with a twist: baseball.

78

HBJ's $50mil renovations included batting cages, a fielding test challenge, and a modern 8,000 seat stadium. The Kansas City Royals inked a 15-year deal for the field to be the team's spring training home where legends like Bo Jackson would hone their skills. Exhibits were borrowed from Cooperstown for the "Taste of Cooperstown" exhibit, and the newly branded Boardwalk and Baseball was ready to play.

Opening in February 1988, Boardwalk and Baseball's commercials promised simpler joys, highlighting their vintage rides, IMAX theater, and baseball experiences, all to a jingle reminding viewers, "there's no such thing as too much fun." Visitors encountered uniform-clad mascots Scooter, Homer, and Specs, the nation's longest log flume, ferris wheels, created their own baseball cards, and were handed a copy of the in-house newspaper *Baseball City Gazette*. In addition was Park Place, a botanical garden intended to give some respite from the noise and rattling rides.

Other than the excitement around the baseball stadium, Boardwalk and Baseball failed to capture the wider public's attention, and HBJ sold the park to Busch Entertainment in 1989 who was in control for less than a year before employees showed up on Jan 17, 1990 to once again find their workplace unceremoniously shuttered. The Royals used the stadium until 2002, and Boardwalk and Baseball was eventually razed to make way for a shopping complex. From the big top to the big leagues, visitors to the various iterations of the theme park in Haines City carry fond memories of simpler times and creative endeavors.

FEATURES AND RIDES

Baseball City Stadium
Batting Cages
The Big Wheel
Bullpen
Bumper Cars
Carousel
Dragon Coaster
Double-O
Faceball Card Studio
Fielding Test
Florida Hurricane
Grand Junction Theatre
Grand Rapid Log Flume
1001 Nights
Santa Maria
Taste of Cooperstown Exhibit
IMAX
Wave Swinger
Super Bowl of Sports Trivia

20

ROADSIDE AMERICA

SHARTLESVILLE, PENNSYLVANIA

1935 - 2020

"The world's greatest indoor miniature village"

Original Publish Date in *ReMIND* Magazine

June, 2024

On a clear summer day in 1903 young Laurence Gieringer and his brother Paul made their way to the top of Mount Penn overlooking the city of Reading, Pennsylvania and were astonished by the clear view of what looked to them like a toy metropolis. The cars, trains, and people were so small, and they could see from one end of town to the other. The pair talked about how fun it would be to re-create such a scene where they could add some of their favorite things. A circus! A waterfall! A parade! The spark ignited in that moment resulted in one of the state's most treasured and long-running attractions: Roadside America.

The boys talked their parents into some space in the living room where

they went to work carving, gluing, and painting as many buildings, characters, and animals as they could crank out after school and on weekends. Seven years later Paul left for the ministry, but Laurence held true to their vision and continued the effort. In 1935 local paper The Reading Eagle caught wind of the layout and featured the Gieringer boys' creation in an article that caught the attention of readers anxious to see the micro marvel. The local fire company offered up a corner in their building to house the growing display, making it available to the public.

Banking on donations, Laurence continued his obsessive expansion which soon mandated even more space, and in 1938 he relocated to a dance hall on the grounds of the Caronia Park amusement complex. By 1940 Laurence had handmade and situated more than 100 buildings among hundreds of human and animal figures with O gauge railroad track weaved throughout. Trains and trolleys made perpetual treks through

beautiful set pieces including mountains and caverns, over bridges, past cemeteries, churches, and coal mines, and through town after town. The layout in its final form consisted of over 17,000ft of lumber, 2,000ft of track, 21,500ft of electric wire, 513 light bulbs, and more than 2,000 gallons of water flowing through its fountains, ponds, streams, and waterfalls.

The final relocation occurred in 1953 when the attraction moved to a building along I-78 and was branded 'Roadside America: The World's Largest Known Indoor Village.' Now at a whopping 8,000sq ft, Laurence, with the help of his kids and grandkids, kept the little burb in tip top shape with regular revisits of paint and glue as thousands of tourists filed through each year to take in the views. Visitors brought binoculars to catch all the detail, could trigger automated scenes with the push of a button, and marveled every thirty minutes at the staged light and sound show when night descended on the display and a multimedia show was projected on the wall celebrating our nation's history to the strains of America the Beautiful.

After Laurence passed away in 1963 his family kept Roadside America humming through 2020 when it fell prey to the COVID pandemic, locking its doors forever. An auction sold off each individual element of the layout, most all to the tune of hundreds of dollars apiece. While the Gieringer boys' labor of love is now dispersed into collector hands around the world, its legacy is legend for all who bore witness to the interactive town-within-a-town in Shartlesville, PA.

DETAILS ON THE ROADSIDE AMERICA DISPLAY

7,450- square feet in size

18 O gauge trains, trolleys, cable cars

10,000 hand-made trees

4,000 miniature people

Real water streams, rivers, and waterways

Animated circus parade, construction sites, saw mill

600 miniature light bulbs

21,500 feet of electrical wiring

17,700 feet of lumber

6,000 feet of building paper

4,000 feet of sheet metal

2.250 feet of railroad track

648 feet of canvas

450 feet of pipe

18,000 pounds of plaster

4,000 pounds of sheet iron

900 pounds of nails

600 pounds of rubber roofing material

75 pounds of dry paint

75 gallons of liquid paint

225 bushels of moss

21

THE ACKERMANSION

LOS ANGELES, CALIFORNIA

Original Publish Date in ReMIND Magazine

July/August, 2024

Forrest J Ackerman was nine years old in the fall of 1929 when two terrifying crustaceans changed his world, and in turn, wound up changing fantasy fandom forever. There before him on a newsstand among the newspapers, celebrity rags, and sports mags sat the October issue of Amazing Stories featuring bold artwork from Frank R. Paul depicting a ravaged man being besieged by two towering lobster creatures in front of a downed spaceship. Ackerman paid his twenty-five cents and raced home, diving into fantastic tales from cover story writer A. Hyatt Verrill, H.G. Wells, and Jules Verne. A spell fell over him.

Forrest J. Ackerman (Photo: James Michael Roddy)

Those 100 pages of thrilling prose led him on a lifelong adventure that culminated 29 years later in *Famous Monsters of Filmland*, his magazine that lifted the veil on the world of genre entertainment with interviews, makeup tutorials, and on-set exclusives, inspiring a generation to try their hand at filmmaking and creating a cult around the man lovingly referred to as "Forry." His screen-used prop and costume-laden home, dubbed "The Ackermansion" quickly became an essential L.A. stop, accessible to anyone who called his oft-published phone number 323-MOONFAN and asked to pay a visit.

Famous Monsters of Filmland's first issue landed in 1958 and quickly became a beacon for "monster kids" with a love for genre entertainment. Among the loyal was young Mick Garris, director behind (among many films) *Sleepwalkers* and Stephen King's *The Stand*, as well as an episode of the 1985 TV series *Amazing Stories* based on the very magazine that started it all for Ackerman.

86

For Garris, it was love at first bite.

"I discovered (*Famous Monsters of Filmland*) at an early age and it was a revelation," the filmmaker relates. "No one cared about monster movies or the fantastic in my town, at least that I knew of. To see this magazine spring up, completely dedicated to one of my greatest passions, was thrill-

Photo: James Michael Roddy

ing. I was suddenly not completely alone."

Gremlins director Joe Dante made a monthly mag rack pilgrimage to track down each new issue of *Famous Monsters* when he was growing up, so enthralled he started writing to Forry. "I would send him letters telling him about movies I was seeing, and the next thing I know my letters started showing up in the magazine as articles," Dante laughs. "Of course, my name wasn't on them, but there they were. My friends and I then started trying to get into those pages as often as we could with our notes to Forry."

Ackerman started publishing his Hollywood Hills address in the magazine, encouraging fans to visit his collection of memorabilia. It was an offer too good to refuse for Jeff Farley, makeup artist behind otherworldly creations in *The Blob* (1988), *Jack-O*, and the Jack Nicholson howler *Wolf*, who first encountered the Ackermansion on a whim.

"My stepmother would take me to the beach during the summer and one day we were driving through Hollywood on the way home. I had Forry's address with me and asked if we could see where he lived. As we drove up Glendower Ave, I saw his orange Cadillac and we decided to stop. (Ackerman secretary) Dennis Billows informed us Forry was in Europe, but let us in anyway and gave us a tour. The experience was incredible."

By 1997 Ackerman estimated more than 25,000 people had been through his halls of horror and sci-fi history, one of which was makeup effects artist Chris Biggs, veteran of *Star Trek, A Nightmare on Elm Street*, and the *Critters* films. "It was a very cool, sort of a California Spanish style three-story house where the top floor was the living space and the second and third floors were all museum," Biggs recalls. "There was so much to look at it was almost overwhelming."

"I'd heard that it was exactly what it turned out to be!" smiles Garris. "A repository of artifacts, props, books, photos, and posters. it was a live-in museum of the fantastic, filled with treasures from the moment you walked in."

Photo: David Del Valle

"The first thing he would show you was Bela Lugosi's ring from *Dracula*," Garris continues, "which he would be wearing. He had an odd, but jolly, sing-song voice and was full joy whenever he was around people."

"In the courtyard was the submarine from George Pal's *Atlantis -The Lost Continent*," shares Farley, who admits there were a few frights, too. "He also had a crawlspace area he called Grislyland where there was a room that contained a large creature from an *Outer Limits* episode and other things. It was dark and a bit scary there."

Film historian David Del Valle became close with Forry over the years, never losing his sense of awe when visiting and talking shop with its iconic caretaker. "The robot from *Metropolis* was the highlight for me," he remembers. "Also, the *King Kong* models."

"The thing that impressed me most," shares Garris, "was (visual effects artist) Willis O'Brien's metal armature from the original *King Kong*. The rubber and fur had long since rotted away, but the posable metal skeleton was amazing to behold."

Not only was Forry a courteous host, but he established long-term friendships with many of his frequent visitors, Jeff Farley among them. "I spent nearly every Saturday there for years," the creature creator relates. "Eventually he made me an unofficial tour guide. His house brought so many people together which led to me having a 50-year career in the industry."

Ackerman with Reggie Nalder and David Del Valle
(Photo: David Del Valle)

Makeup effects icon Rick Baker was among the many who would regularly drop items off to add to the collection, as did Chris Biggs, who shares, "I gave him the giant bug monster's head from *Critters 2*, some dead aliens, and a few other things." It was an ever-expanding menagerie that inspired everyone who passed through, an extension of the influence Ackerman's magazine offered.

"There was no horror fandom before *Famous Monsters of Filmland*," Garris reflects. "Forry is responsible for nurturing and bonding creative outsiders. A generation of our greatest filmmakers consumed the magazine in their wonder years, and his encouragement in print changed everything. The Ackermansion was the Disneyland of Monsters, a home for those outsiders who dreamed nightmares and created nightmares on the screen. To us oddball monster lovers, it was home."

Much of Ackerman's collection, that he once estimated at totaling more than 300,000 pieces, now resides at the Motion Picture Museum, preserved for all time. And you don't have to call ahead to pay them a visit.

MICK GARRIS FULL INTERVIEW

Justin Beahm: When did you discover *Famous Monsters* magazine, and what did it mean to you?

Mick Garris: I discovered it at a very early age. Maybe 11 or so? And it was a revelation. No one I knew cared about monster movies or the fantastic in my school or my town… at least that I knew of. And I was very much a loner kid, so I was used to feeling alone in my popular culture attractions. And to see this magazine spring up in front of me, dedicated completely to one of my greatest passions, was thrilling. I was suddenly not completely alone.

JB: When did you first learn about the Ackermansion and what did you hear about it?

MG: I'd always heard that it existed, reading about it in the magazine, of course. I'd heard that it was exactly what it turned out to be! A repository of artifacts, props, books, photos, posters from the world of horror

Mick Garris in promotional photo

and monsters. I never thought I'd ever get the chance to see it in person!

JB: Tell us what led to your first visit, and tell us about that initial experience

MG: I found out that at that time, maybe late 1970's, Forry would welcome visitors to see his home: all they had to do was call is number, which he didn't bother to keep secret: 323-MOONFAN. So a couple friends who knew him took me to see that house on Glendower, and it was not a disappointment! It was a live-in museum of the fantastic. Later, I got to know him and the Ackermansion better when I was doing genre publicity for Avco-Embassy, and I had arranged an event with the genre press to promote John Carpenter's *The Fog*, and we held the press conference at the Ackermansion, which Forry was more that willing to host.

JB: Describe the house and what you encountered in it

MG: The house is a beautiful example of 1920's Hollywood Spanish style architecture. It was old—in the California sense—but filled with amazing treasures from the moment you walked into it. Genre passion was not then what it is today. Horror conventions and film festivals were rare, and autograph-hound fandom almost nonexistent. But it was like being embraced by Tod Browning's *Freaks*. Gooble gobble, one of us!

JB: Describe Forry and how he interacted with visitors

MG: There's no question that Forry was eccentric. I interacted with him many times over the years, and I always got the feeling that he didn't remember me, until much later in his life. He had an odd—but jolly—sing song voice and a full joy whenever he was around people. And almost always, the first thing he would do would be to show you Bela Lugosi's ring from *Dracula*, which Forry himself was wearing. He always seemed to be having fun, but he was also like the weird uncle most of us have.

JB: What were your favorite things Forry had there?

MG: The thing that impressed me the most in Forry's collection was Willis O'Brian's metal armature from the original *King Kong*. The rubber and fur had long since rotted away, but the posable metal skeleton was amazing to behold.

JB: Tell us about your discussions with Forry over the years and what your relationship was like.

MG: Though Forry was always a gentleman, and always eager to talk, I think he was a hard guy to get close to. I never really talked to him about anything but the movies, which were obviously his greatest love. Later on in the 90s, he would remember me and we would talk about monsters and movies—usually old movies; I don't think he had much interest in the newer films that were coming out—and he was charming and funny and, like so many who've devoted their lives to movie monsters, a little weird… but in a good way.

JB: How would you describe Forry's legacy and how does his house play into that?

MG: Well, there was no horror fandom to speak of before Forry founded *Famous Monsters of Filmland*. Forry is responsible for nurturing and bonding creative outsiders, people who felt alone in their passions. A generation of our greatest filmmakers consumed *Famous Monsters* in their wonder years, and this encouragement in print changed everything. Horror fandom now had a home that brought us all together, all across the country. And the Ackermansion—to some spooky, but to me delightful, was the Disneyland of Monsters, a home for those outsiders and weirdos who dreamed nightmares, and created nightmares to share with them on the screen. To many of us oddball monster lovers, it was home.

Ferdy Mayne with Ackerman (Photo: David Del Valle)

JEFF FARLEY FULL INTERVIEW

Justin Beahm: When did you discover *Famous Monsters* magazine, and what did it mean to you as a kid?

Jeff Farley: I first encountered the *FM* 1972 Fearbook in a local Liquor Store in my hometown of La Crescenta, CA. I was hooked immediately.

JB: When did you first learn about the Ackermansion and what did you hear about it?

JF: Forry would publish his address in various issues as well as photos and that gave me an impression of what the Ackermansion was like. This was his second home/museum in the los Feliz area of the Hollywood Hills.

JB: Tell us what led to your first visit, and tell us about that initial experience.

JF: My stepmother would take my sister and I to the beach during the summers and we would drive through Hollywood on the way home.

Ackerman with Jeff Farley (Photo: Jeff Farley)

I had Forry's address with me and I asked her if we could go by and see where he lived. As we drove up the street he lived on, Glendower Ave., I saw his orange Cadillac and we decided to stop. When we inquired through an intercom, Dennis Billows answered, telling us Forry was in Europe but he let us in anyway and gave us a tour. For a kid like me, the experience was incredible. Rooms full of film history, thousands of books as well as art, it seemed as though it went on forever. A footnote to this story is that a friend of my stepmother's was also working for Forry at the time and it was the first time they had seen each other in a while.

JB: Describe the house and everything you encountered in it.

JF: The house was a large Spanish-style multi-story home with steps that led down the side of the garage and those led to his office/museum.

In the courtyard was the submarine from George Pal's *Atlantis - The Lost Continent*. Each room was filled with amazing memorabilia. There were so many pieces that it is impossible to describe everything.

JB: Describe Forry and how he interacted with visitors/kids.

JF: Forry was a kind man with endless curiosity. He would take the time to listen and treated everyone I saw there with complete respect…children & adults alike. One personal interaction involved a day my (late) friend Arlin Teeselink and I visiting one day while a film crew was there. As Forry, Arlin and I were talking, the crew was filming us and after they moved to another area, Forry says to us, "Well, it looks like you are going to appear on (West) German TV. He loved having visitors.

JB: You have said you ended visiting a lot. Tell us how often, what you would do during the visits, and how the place changed over time.

JF: After the first visit, it was Forry who called me one night after he had returned from Europe and had heard I had a Birthday coming up and invited me over. A couple of my friends were also invited and we had a wonderful day there. John Landis showed up and gave us a lot of information on a film that would take him a few more years to get off the ground, *An American Werewolf in London*. Afterward, I would take a couple of buses from my place to his on Saturdays when he would have his open-houses and I spent nearly every Saturday there for three years. There weren't many changes in the time I visited. Maybe a new piece for the collection from time-to-time.

JB: What were your favorite things Forry had there?

JF: I have always been a fan of stop motion and seeing the actual models from Willis O'Brien's *King Kong* and a few of Ray Harryhausen's films was a treat I never thought I would experience.

JB: Did he ever show you things that were normally hidden from public view?

JF: He had a crawlspace area he called Grislyland and that was a room which contained a large creature from an *Outer Limits* episode as well as a few other items. It was dark and a bit scary under there. He would show people that area from time-to-time and eventually, he made me an unofficial tour guide and it was my job to take new guests there.

JB: How did the time spent at the Ackermansion lead to you getting into the business?

JF: Forry called one night to invite me to meet Ray Harryhausen on New Years Eve in 1976. There was another guy named Douglas Barrett Jones there and he had been working at Don Post & The Burman Studios and it was soon after meeting him that night that he contacted me to help with background tarantula props for *Kingdom of the Spiders*. That led to a nearly 50 year career in the film industry as a Special Effects Makeup Artist.

JB: Tell us about your last time visiting.

JF: It must have been in the '90's that I was able to make it back and everything was still in place though there were a few cobwebs.

JB: How would you describe Forry's legacy and how does his house play into that?

JF: Forry had given so much of his free time to myself and many others. His selfless nature and knowledge has been passed on and there will never be another like him. His house and museum brought so many people together, made them lifelong friends and his generosity will always be remembered by those of us lucky to have known him.

Photo: James Michael Roddy

22

HAGENBECK-WALLACE CIRCUS

PERU, INDIANA

1882 - 1938

Original Publish Date in *ReMIND* Magazine

September, 2024

In 1882 Peru, Indiana-based horse trader and animal trainer Benjamin Wallace attended the bankruptcy sale of the W.C. Coup Circus in Wisconsin, returning with seven train cars full of tents, poles, costumes, and equipment. Similar auctions in Texas and Chicago yielded a variety of animals and wagons he set about restoring. Two years later, after assembling a roster of the best perform-

ers he could find, the Wallace and Co.'s Great World Menagerie presented its first performance in its hometown and started touring soon thereafter. The show would eventually blossom into the nation's third largest circus but is now best remembered for suffering a string of unimaginable tragedies.

By 1885 The Menagerie was a one-ring show traversing Indiana, Ohio,

West Virginia, and Kentucky by twenty-six horse drawn wagons. In 1886 Wallace transitioned to rail travel, coasting into towns with an impressive forty freight and wagon cars carrying his expanding roster of animals, a cookhouse, sleeping quarters for performers, and his array of tents. While the growing network of railroad routes allowed Wallace to expand into a national presence, the show's base remained in Indiana where it found home on a 220-acre farm for winter quarters.

In July of 1892 the first blow hit the Wallace show when a train derailment killed twenty-six of his performance horses. Eleven years and hundreds of shows later in August 1903, horror once again visited the troupe when a train carrying half of the show's cars failed to stop as it entered a railyard behind the first half, an accident that took the lives

Photos: Library of Congress

97

of twenty-six performers, several dozen rail workers, and some animals. It was the worst circus train crash on record until fifteen years later when the darkest of days befell the plagued variety show one last time.

In 1907 Wallace re-branded his show The Hagenbeck-Wallace Circus after purchasing the Chicago-based Carl Hagenbeck Circus. Promoted as a "high class" family experience, Wallace was greeted in town after town by cheering crowds and packed houses. Continuing their unfortunate trend, six years later a flood took out eight elephants, twenty-one lions and tigers, and eight horses, which led to Wallace selling his show. But the worst was yet to come.

On June 22, 1918, New York Central Railroad #8485, a troop transport train empty after finishing dropping its inhabitants in Kalamazoo, Michigan, was making a nocturnal trek to Chicago to pick up more enlistees when its engineer fell asleep, leaving the train unattended and speeding along

Photos: Library of Congress

the tracks at twenty-five miles per hour. Just ahead, hobbled by a problem car at a switchover point near Hammond, Indiana, was one of the long Hagenbeck-Wallace trains, stationary on the same track.

The circus train cars disintegrated as the 150-ton New York Central cut through them like a knife, initiating a fire, killing 86 people, and setting a regretful benchmark as the deadliest circus rail accident in history. The incident ended a nightmarish streak of thrilling highs and harrowing lows for one of the nation's most celebrated shows.

Photos: Library of Congress

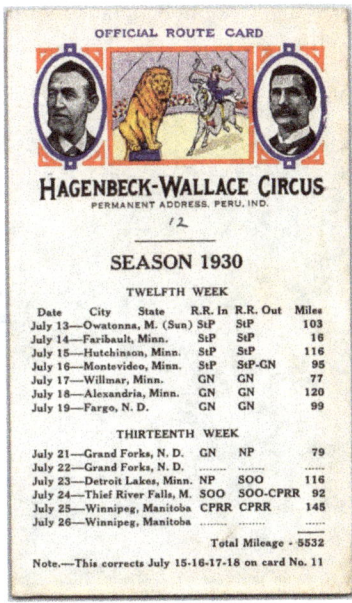

OFFICIAL ROUTE CARD

HAGENBECK-WALLACE CIRCUS
PERMANENT ADDRESS, PERU, IND.

12

SEASON 1930

TWELFTH WEEK

Date	City	State	R.R. In	R.R. Out	Miles
July 13—Owatonna, M. (Sun)			StP	StP	103
July 14—Faribault, Minn.			StP	StP	16
July 15—Hutchinson, Minn.			StP	StP	116
July 16—Montevideo, Minn.			StP	StP-GN	95
July 17—Willmar, Minn.			GN	GN	77
July 18—Alexandria, Minn.			GN	GN	120
July 19—Fargo, N. D.			GN	GN	99

THIRTEENTH WEEK

July 21—Grand Forks, N. D.			GN	NP	79
July 22—Grand Forks, N. D.			....	....	......
July 23—Detroit Lakes, Minn.			NP	SOO	116
July 24—Thief River Falls, M.			SOO	SOO-CPRR	92
July 25—Winnipeg, Manitoba			CPRR	CPRR	145
July 26—Winnipeg, Manitoba			....	....	......

Total Mileage - 5532

Note.—This corrects July 15-16-17-18 on card No. 11

99

THE HAGENBECK-WALLACE CIRCUS IN MINIATURE AT HOUSE ON THE ROCK IN SPRING GREEN, WISCONSIN

The House on the Rock in Spring Green, Wisconsin is the brainchild of Alex Jordan, an accidental architect who hand-built his dream home atop Deer

The House on the Rock

Shelter Rock, a 60-foot tower of sandstone in the wilds of Central Wisconsin. Jordan poured his love for international style, art, and artifacts into the unconventional 13-room abode that boasts a strong Eastern influence in layout and materials and eventually included the

house's signature feature: the Infinity Room, and arrow-shaped protrusion that extends 218-feet from the house, seemingly floating in air 140-feet above the valley below.

Jordan eventually opened his home to the public and started adding buildings to the property to house his singular collection of artifacts from around the world that includes armor, jeweled crowns, ancient weaponry, historical nautical artifacts, unique vehicles, automated mannequin musicians, the world's largest carousel, a massive true-to-scale blue whale, airplanes, the Streets of Yesteryear, an elaborately detailed vintage city street, and many creations born of his own imagination. House on the Rock instantly became a signature attraction in the Badger state and remains so to this

A segment of the Hagenbeck-Wallace Circus display

day.

A trip to House on The Rock is a wonderful, if overwhelming, experience that begins with a walk through the namesake house, then moves on to other "houses" that are packed with increasingly incredible sights so densely populated with fascinating oddities that you can visit over and over and always find new things to be wowed by.

The trapeze section of the display

One of the tour segments is The Circus Building, and in addition to a life-sized pyramid of elephants, includes a celebration of the Hagenbeck-Wallace Circus done in miniature. The detail of the assembly is incredible, said to include more than one million pieces in all. The presentation is of a lively day under the big top with clowns, wagons, train cars, trapeze and sideshow performers, gymnasts, animals, and all the trappings one would have encountered in a real-life visit to the show. Jordan was said to have been enamored of the Hagenbeck-Wallace Circus after attending in his youth, and this tiny tribute to what once was the biggest show on Earth is worth the price of admission to The House on the Rock in itself.

The House on the Rock's Infinity Room

23

THE HAUNTED MONSTER MUSEUM

NATURAL BRIDGE, VIRGINIA

1982 - 2012

Original Publish Date in *ReMIND* Magazine

October, 2024

Mark Cline was born a dreamer. From the beginning he was a creative standout in his hometown of Waynesboro, Virginia where he made the local paper in 1968 at age 7 after winning a snowman contest with his take on the Statue of Liberty. He got further attention in 6th grade for his comic strip "Adventures with George," and was known for backyard film adventures, which included his portrayal of "Superboy." Cline's life path was cemented at age 12

Photos: Mark Cline

when he happened upon the magnificent creations at Dinosaur Land in White Post, VA, prompting him to tell his dad he would one day make such things himself. That is exactly what he did.

After high school Cline traveled the U.S. by river and motorcycle, making a living taking photos of tourists posing on his bike next to his two-headed biker sculpture. He eventually returned to Waynesboro where he looked for creative work, including pitching city officials on a sculpture of town namesake Mad Anthony Wayne, which was met with disregard.

The artist relocated to Natural Bridge, VA in 1982 and opened The Monster Museum on Route 11 where passersby could thrill to Cline's ghoulish creations. The endeavor was less than successful, and Cline was in financial straits by 1984, a situation that literally drove the despondent creature maker to the edge where an epiphany led him on a new mission: to simply make people happy.

In 1985 Cline re-tooled The Monster Museum, removing many beasties and replacing them with more majestic and silly creations. The Enchanted Castle offered travelers the chance to sit on the lap of a 10ft tick, get zapped to Venus, sink on the Titanic, and watch a pig bungee jump. The tour also included a

Photos: Mark Cline

trip through Cline's workshop where visitors could watch him sculpt.

Cline soon started getting commissioned to create statues for mini golf courses, haunted houses, and attractions including Six Flags and the Jellystone Park campground chain. Particularly popular were his dinosaurs, which eventually included an installation at Dinosaur Land, the park that started it all.

In 1997 Cline teamed up with a struggling local baseball team with a mock seance to counter that season's misfortunes. This put Cline on the radar of conservative groups who branded his Museum the work of Satan, and on April 9, 2001, he found his Enchanted Castle engulfed in flames. In the mailbox was a letter admonishing, "...fire represents God's judgement. Behold - the Judge is standing at the door."

One year later Natural Bridge gifted Cline an abandoned mansion to rebuild and The Haunted Monster Museum opened months later, populated with a diverse lineup of new creations including skeletons of the Marx Brothers, a 15ft Frankenchicken, seance room, and more. The success of his dino commissions led Cline to create Dinosaur Kingdom in front of the Monster Museum, where tourists wandered about towering prehistoric creatures doing battle with Civil War soldiers. In 2005 Cline added Foamhenge, a life size reproduction of Stonehenge.

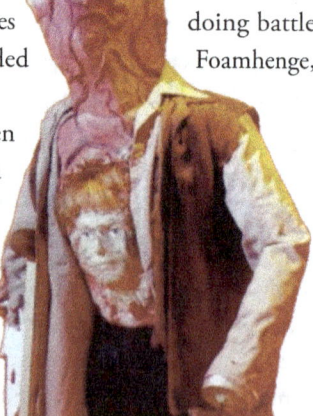

Tragedy once again struck in 2012 when the Haunted Monster Museum repeated history, burning to the ground and taking many dinosaurs with it. Ever the entertainer, Cline now hosts ghost tours in Lexington and runs the newly opened Dinosaur Kingdom II.

24

LUDLOW LAGOON

LUDLOW, KENTUCKY

1895 - 1917

"The handsomest park on Earth"

Original Publish Date in *ReMIND* Magazine

November/December, 2024

Ludlow, Kentucky is situated just west of Cincinnati, Ohio, and in the early 1800s The Green Line streetcar company was the area's main form of public transportation. In 1894, in effort to bolster tourism and give locals a recreational destination, the town dammed Pleasant Run Creek at the end of the Ludlow streetcar line, creating an 85-acre lagoon that included five small islands. Developer JJ Weaver was put in charge of evolving the space.

Cincinnati architect John Boll designed a grand chateau-like entrance to greet Lagoon visitors. Beyond the entrance was a grass parkway leading to the lake and the centerpiece of the park's activity, the clubhouse. Boasting a restaurant, billiard room, and wrap-around veranda offering breathtaking views of the lake, the Victorian inspired building became a gathering place for visitors and area elites after the Lagoon opened in 1895.

The Green Line appointed a trolley dubbed "The Dinky" to make trips to and from the Lagoon throughout the day, always packed with folks looking to relax on the beach, enjoy live jazz at the dance pavilion, try their hand at midway games, or take a dip in the lake's clear waters. Soon a 100-foot Ferris wheel was added, followed by a suspended swing ride, an exhibition of Thomas Edison inventions, and Chute-The-Chutes.

Chute-the-Chutes was the invention of designer Paul Boyton and an early version of what we now refer to as a log ride. Passengers boarded a boat situated atop a ramp, and careened toward the lake where they would splash down and rocket across the water's surface. Traveling at speeds up to 37 miles per hour, Chute-the-Chutes was as thrilling as it was dangerous,

and after frequent rider injuries the attraction was removed.

Designer LaMarcus Thompson brought his Scenic Railway roller coaster design from New York's Coney Island to Ludlow, creating a dramatic rise and fall route over the lake that would circle back on itself inside a turnaround building. An arial roadway offered the chance to drive a Buick automobile through the treetops around the park and was notable as an early chance for women to get behind the wheel at a time when that was rare.

JJ Weaver continued to add attractions including a miniature railroad, hot air balloon rides, and an outdoor amphitheater. In 1898 when the Spanish American war broke out, the park welcomed a Cuban refugee family to move to one of its islands where a "traditional Cuban farm" was built for them, all in effort to exhibit what Caribbean life was like.

Lights illuminated the park at night at a time when electricity was still scarce. In 1913 a circular motordrome track was added. A few months

after opening, celebrated cycler Odin Johnson blew a tire during a race which sent him and his bike into a wire mesh barrier between the track and spectators, hitting a lamp post that sent burning oil into the stands, initiating a massive blaze that left 10 dead and 100s injured. Soon thereafter a flood damaged several buildings, and in 1915 a tornado levelled many park structures.

Crippled by these tragedies, the Ludlow Lagoon closed and was razed in 1917. The space continued to be a hub of activity for fishing, boating, winter ice skating, and recreation for decades after.

Cincinnati Tornado, July 7th, 1915.
Ruins of the Lagoon Motor Drome.

FEATURES AND RIDES

Autoing in the Treetops
Motordrome
Theater
Scenic Railway
Clubhouse
Boathouse
Shooting the Chutes
Boat Rides
Amphitheater
Hot Air Balloon Rides
Miniature Railroad
Traditional Cuban Farm
Dance Pavillion
Beachfront

25

COOPERSTOWN

PHOENIX, ARIZONA

1998 - 2017

"Where rock & jocks meet"

Original Publish Date in *ReMIND* Magazine

January, 2025

Alice Cooper is a man of many guises. He is a music icon and artistic chameleon, having transitioned from creepy psychedelic rock and roll to polished hair metal and beyond over the course of his storied career. He is an avid golfer, never missing early morning tee time wherever he gigs. He is a devoted parent and grandparent, priding himself on sticking to sobriety since 1983 so he could be the family man he had always intended to be. He is also a sports obsessive, a passion he blended with entrepreneurial zeal when he opened a restaurant called Cooperstown in Phoenix, Arizona in late 1998.

The concept was to create a space, "where jocks and rock meet," as promotional flyers trumpeted in advance of the restaurant's December grand opening. Cooperstown was to be a riff on what the Hard Rock Cafe had done around the country, offering a dining experience in the midst of genuine memorabilia from the worlds of music, baseball, football, and hockey. It was the most demanding project the legendary shock rocker had even embarked on.

"Getting a tour together is about a hundred times easier than putting a restaurant together," Cooper said to media as doors opened for the first time. The space occupied a building on Jackson Street in Phoenix's warehouse district just a stone's throw from Bank One Ballpark (now Chase Field) where the Arizona Diamondbacks played. The endeavor was 100% Alice, who was hands-on with every aspect from the decor to the menu.

Packed with creative dishes named after athletes and musicians, the Cooperstown menu offered "The Big Unit" hot dog, named after all-star pitcher Randy Johnson, quarterback Kurt Warner's corned beef sandwich, Bo Diddley's blues burger, which promised a feast of melted bleu cheese and crispy hickory bacon, and

110

Sheryl Coopers veggie quesadilla, named after his wife and creative partner. Everything on the menu had a gimmick, some related to Alice's musical catalog ("nightmare" chili), some related to newer performers, as was the case with Lady Gaga's hot

links.

On the walls was a dazzling assortment of autographed instruments, stage and music video-worn costumes, signed jerseys, artwork, and memorabilia from throughout Cooper's career. For visitors it was an opportunity to get

Signed guitars at Cooperstown (Photo: Travis Shepherd)

up close with music and sports history, and for the restaurant's proprietor it was a chance to also give back to fans and the community, offering a similarly unforgettable experience to what his concerts had been delivering for decades in addition to charity and food hand-out events.

"I don't want there to be one in every mall," the veteran entertainer shared with media on the day ground was first broken. "It's something I always wanted to do. I want it to be Alice's legacy."

Cooperstown would grow to three locations, each offering different memorabilia in addition to keepsakes like baseballs, jerseys, and guitar picks in addition to live music and special events. Denver opened in 2001 and lasted just a year before shuttering, Cleveland opened in 2002 and left Cooper's ownership in 2007. The flagship Phoenix location lasted two decades until 2017 before permanently closing.

Stage-worn straightjacket signed by Alice (Photo: Travis Shepherd)

Cooper's legacy is cemented in his massive musical shadow, and while the 2011 Rock and Roll Hall of Fame inductee has not returned to the world of burgers and beers since Cooperstown left the stage in 2017, those who dined there carry forth great memories of a truly unique experiment in blending cultural realms.

26

20,000 LEAGUES UNDER THE SEA SUBMARINE VOYAGE

LAKE BUENA VISTA, FLORIDA

1971 - 1994

"Relive Captain Nemo's adventures...journey through liquid space!"

Original Publish Date in *ReMIND* Magazine

February, 2025

In 1958, three years after opening to great fanfare, Disneyland in Anaheim, California was buzzing with inventive concepts for new attractions in effort to continue their amusement park revolution. Walt's team of creatives dreamt up The Submarine Voyage, an immersive 1,365ft long lagoon journey inside a partially submerged rail-guided submarine where riders would move through a ship graveyard, skirt the North Pole, head to the bottom of the sea, coast through Atlantis, and encounter a sea serpent before "surfacing." It was a hit, and when plans began for Disney's expansion into a sister park in Florida, the team set their sights on an expanded Submarine experience and found inspiration in one of the studio's most popular films, *20,000 Leagues Under the Sea* (1954).

Based on the novel by Jules Verne, the film follows Kirk Douglas as Ned Land, a sailor on a ship that falls prey to a rumored sea monster, only to end up inside the beast, which turns out to be an elaborate submarine captained by a madman named Captain Nemo (James Mason). The film may have been anchored by two of the era's biggest actors, but the real star

was The Nautilus, Nemo's endlessly ornate technologically advanced sub that captured the imaginations of viewers young and old. Disney wanted his new ride, set to premiere on opening day of Walt Disney World's Magic Kingdom in Bay Lake, Florida in 1971, to closely replicate what the world saw on film.

The *20,000 Leagues Under the Sea* Submarine Voyage featured 13 subs that each held 38 passengers, guided on a track through 11mil gallons of water in a lagoon through familiar scenes from the movie. The film's Nautilus design was employed, and Morgan Yachts in Clearwater, Florida tackled initial construction, which was finished by Tampa Ship, who delivered the boats to Magic Kingdom in August 1971. The project ran

over budget, but the results were worth the extra expense, as evinced by long lines from the start.

Riders boarded and sat down to peer out individual portholes under the surface of the water. Once the boat left dock, bubbles obscured the view, suggesting descent. With Nemo's organ music providing an underscore, patrons were then greeted by beautiful scenery including lobsters, turtles, fish, and eels, as the Captain's voice guided them. They then encountered a storm before moving through a ship graveyard, the North Pole, and Atlantis, same as on the ride's California counterpart. The main event came in the form of a giant squid "attacking" the subs, replicating the film's centerpiece encounter.

The ride was the park's most expensive to operate, necessitating 20 employees and constant maintenance battling the water and elements. Despite enduring patron interest, it was announced in 1994 that *20,000 Leagues* would be temporarily closed for maintenance, but the attraction never re-opened. It was eventually razed, its four acres twice replaced with new construction since. All but two of the famous Nautilus submarines were buried in a plot of land on the park's outskirts, the survivors moved to Disney's private island

Castaway Cay in 2000 where they remind divers of one of the amusement industry's most memorable experiences.

27

THE CALIFORNIA ALLIGATOR FARM

LOS ANGELES, CALIFORNIA

1907 - 1984

"World's largest alligator farm"

Original Publish Date in *ReMIND* Magazine

February, 2025

Joseph Campbell was dubbed "Alligator Joe" when he opened a gator farm in Hot Springs, Arkansas in 1906. Campbell had recently relocated from India and established himself as a showman in the Hot Springs area, which caught the eye of California ostrich farmer Francis Earnest, who convinced Campbell there was more money to be made in the West. In 1907 the duo boarded a train, along with four dozen reptilians, and made

their way to Los Angeles where they planned a new attraction next to Earnest's farm in the Lincoln Heights neighborhood. A banner hung from the side of the train promoting their vision: The California Alligator Farm.

Campbell and Earnest set up enclosures and a pond to house their ancient menagerie, which quickly blossomed in population to more than 1,000 gators. Turtles, iguanas, cobras, mambas, and pythons were soon added, and word spread fast about L.A.'s popular new attraction. Among the mass of monsters was "Billy," the most famous of all the farm's residents who went on to appear in more than 500 films, commanding $100 a day for his performances.

For $.25 patrons got to wander among the gators, watch them eat live chickens and bear witness to workers wrestling with the beasts. Throughout the day some of the gators would be prompted to climb a ramp and cruise down

a 16ft tall slide into a pond where their annoyed brethren would snap and roar as they hit the water. Visitors could also adopt a baby gator, and even exchange it when it grew too big.

Most shockingly, the attraction's signature offering was the opportunity to have children ride around the park on gators fitted with saddles, something promoted on postcards that circulated around the world. Visitors could stop by the gift shop and pick up alligator skin handbags, wallets, and shoes crafted from the hides of the creatures they had paid to visit.

While turnstiles roared to the tune of more than 100,000 annual visitors at the attraction's peak, running the farm was complicated. Alligators ate up to 15lbs of meat a week and would hibernate between November

and May, burying themselves in silt and not eating for months at a time. It became a rite of passage for local college students to steal gators under the cover of night, and when it would rain too much the lagoon would flood, offering its inhabitants

117

2275 – "TEX", THE TRAINER, ALLIGATOR FARM, LOS ANGELES, CALIFORNIA.

an open door to float into the neighborhood and wander. Then there were the injuries.

Tour guide Alonzo "Tex" Hartzel was bitten and almost killed by a rattlesnake while giving a tour in 1910. Tex also suffered an attack courtesy of the jaws of "Evangeline," the farm's largest gator, later that same year during a photo shoot. Ken Earnest, grandson of Francis, inherited the farm and moved it to Buena Vista in 1953. Ken would suffer bites from four snakes over time, which took sight from one of his eyes and rendered an arm paralyzed. He was also bitten by geriatric gator "Salty" which necessitated a long row of stitches in his leg.

Despite the escapes, injuries, and thievery, The California Alligator Farm entertained until 1984 when public interest dwindled, and the attraction closed, and the gators were moved to Florida. While the farm is no more, the echoes of heart stopping encounters there continue to resonate to this day.

Acknowledgments

Thanks to Lynn Amacher, my creative co-pilot. Lynn's contributions to all of my work, from film to my website and on to this book, cannot be celebrated enough. This whole project was Lynn's suggestion, and he was instrumental in its design from top to bottom. I owe him more than I can ever repay.

Thanks to Barb Oates at NTVB/*ReMIND* who has nurtured the Roadside Memories column over the years and who kindly wrote the beautiful forward to this book. Barb is a kind heart, creative spirit, and I am honored to get the opportunity to partner with her on projects like this.

Thanks to NTVB and *TVGuide* for rolling the dice with that all-*Halloween* issue back in 2021 and for their continued support of Roadside Memories.

Thanks to Mike Ankener for first bringing me into the fold and for the many great conversations over time.

Thanks to my family: Julian, Mom, Dad, and Mitch for their love, patience, and support.

Thanks to everyone who contributed to these stories, including Jeff Farley, Chris Biggs, Mick Garris, James Michael Roddy, David Del Valle, Alice Cooper, Travis Shepherd, Raymond Castile, and the guy who helped me get into Ghost Town in the Sky when it was abandoned and gave me a personal tour, complete with tales from his years as a performer in the cowboy shootout that happened every hour in the park. I am sorry to have lost track of your name.

Thanks to Shane Bundy and Greg Morgan for subscribing to *ReMIND* just to get my column, and for being incredible friends.

Thanks to Uncle Rudy "Dude" Strasser who taught me it is okay to do creative things in addition to the daily grind. He had no idea how much of an impact he and his accordion had on me and how powerful his lessons would be about the importance of the hustle.

Thanks to Grandma Margaret Beahm, an eternal artist who always wanted to read whatever I wrote, hear about my hockey games, and who never slowed down until mother nature forced her to.

Thank you, reader, for spending some time with Roadside Memories. Remember to record, archive, and celebrate those around you and invest in the preservation of their stories and your own.

www.ingramcontent.com/pod-product-compliance
Lightning Source LLC
Chambersburg PA
CBHW070752120626
46557CB00002B/553